"This book is a must-read for anyone working with youth—and anyone truly committed to creating a generation of young leaders who are capable of taking on the complex issues facing the world today. The resounding point of the book is that those people who believe that our youth are the leaders of tomorrow are procrastinating."

    —Kate Cumbo, Ph.D., Program Director
    PeaceJam Foundation, Arvada, CO

"'Someday, when you're in the real world,' is a familiar refrain to young people. But these authors believe in the capacity of young people to be leaders of today, as well as their potential to be leaders of tomorrow. *Giving Voice to the Leader Within* addresses the crucial tensions between guidance, inspiration, facilitation, and direction, as young people develop their power to lead and serve. Diverse young voices are highlighted in each chapter through stories that anticipate the spirit and values of a new generation of leaders. And each chapter ends with reflections and actions to help adults know when to step in, step up, or step out of the way."

    —Mike Klein, Social Justice Vocations Instructor
    Justice and Peace Studies, University of St. Thomas, St. Paul, MN

"The Minnesota young people and adults who attended the 1997 Presidents' Summit for America's Future in Philadelphia sparked development of a distinctive state approach that has inspired the nation. *Giving Voice to the Leader Within* brilliantly captures key elements of Minnesota's youth–adult partnership model and the role of adults working 'with' young people versus 'for' them. Readers will find these lively real-life stories with lessons learned encouraging and instructive."

    —Jim Kielsmeier, Ph.D., Founder and CEO
    National Youth Leadership Council, St. Paul, MN

"For those of us who advocate and encourage the inclusion of youth in governance and civic engagement, there is probably no better guide than this to bringing in the youth, making them feel welcome and comfortable in their role. We all need to hear what they are thinking and what they know. *Giving Voice* can help us support young people in making their voices heard."

    —Ellis Bullock, Executive Director
    Grotto Foundation, Minneapolis, MN

Giving Voice to the Leader Within

Practical Ideas and Actions
for Parents and Adults
Who Work with Young People

Donna C. Gillen
Marlys C. Johnson
&
Jackie S. Sinykin

SYREN BOOK COMPANY
MINNEAPOLIS

Most Syren books are available at special quantity discounts for bulk purchases for sales promotions, premiums, fund-raising, and educational needs. For details, write

Syren Book Company
Special Sales Department
5120 Cedar Lake Road
Minneapolis, MN 55416

Published by
Syren Book Company
5120 Cedar Lake Road
Minneapolis, MN 55416

Printed in the United States of America on acid-free paper

ISBN-13: 978-0-929636-69-6
ISBN-10: 0-929636-69-4

LCCN: 2006933303

Cover design by Kyle G. Hunter
Book design by Wendy Holdman
Photography by Heather M. Gillen

To order additional copies of this book see the form at the back of this book or go to www.itascabooks.com

The Voice of Young People

Youth will not be forgotten!
We care too much to let that happen.
We, the citizen leaders of not only tomorrow, but today
are here to actively express, plan, and implement our ideas in partnerships
    with our communities.
Together, youth and adults are the stakeholders in this society.
We must all be at the table.
Not only will our presence be recognized,
but our values will be heard,
and our actions will be felt in every community.
Together we are strong.
We are here to stand up to the problems and be the solutions.
Through meaningful communication and action,
We are ready to partner with our world and to start sharing.
We are ready to leave our comfort zones and to learn.

Becky Jarvis, Youth Co-chair, Minnesota Alliance with Youth
April 24, 1998

Contents

Introduction

Beginning the Journey

The three of us—Donna, Jackie, and Marlys—have known each other over a period of twenty years. We have served together on a variety of statewide (Minnesota) boards and commissions and have been active in many of the same organizations. We have long respected and valued each other's perspectives and skills.

Over the past decade, and more, we have been thrilled by the growing number of organizations that are involving youth on boards, committees, and in other leadership positions. At the same time, we have been disappointed that a number of people, with good hearts and good intentions, don't understand how— once the young people are invited to serve—to engage them equally and effectively. Many young people, for example, are the only youth voice on a board and are often intimidated when asked, after listening to a long discussion, "Well, what does our youth representative think?" The young person is put into the spotlight without the benefit of participating in the conversation and with the expectation that what he or she thinks, all young people think. At other times, in a rush to complete an agenda, young voices are cut off. Quite a conundrum!

Our belief is that every young person has the capacity for leadership, but it doesn't always emerge naturally or "on the spot." We've seen young people, who were touched by adults and engaged as equals, grow in leadership, discover their talents, and learn to express them. The biggest issue seems to be time. We are so busy with our own lives that setting aside the time required to fully engage young people is often overwhelming. This challenging work does take time—and lots of it.

Knowing that youth need a caring adult to develop their leadership capacities, we decided to explore a project that would capture our combined experiences with young people and be valuable to others, one that we could work on together. With the support of another colleague, Joyce Johannson, who facilitated our initial discussion, we discovered that our passion intersected around youth, leadership, and service because service provides a natural, practical, and dynamic process for building leadership.

As an outgrowth of that first exchange of ideas, we decided to create a book that would be more than just something to read, but a book that the reader could *use*. Marlys was to be the writer; Donna and Jackie, the interviewers and gatherers of information and stories. Throughout the project, we regularly sat together to share our own life stories and our experiences with young people. As Donna says, "We poured out our souls—who we are—with young people." The result is now before you in this book: *Giving Voice to the Leader Within*.

In our early, sometimes heated, other times hilarious, explorations, clarity came when we identified that young people are looking for support, opportunities, space, and resources to become leaders and contributors—thus the primary chapters in this book. Each chapter, including the introductory one on leadership, uses ideas and stories to illustrate the underlying value proposition. At the end of each chapter we have included suggestions for personal reflection and leadership activities to be done with young people.

The thought-provoking reflections encourage readers to think back on their own experiences and assess the impact those experiences had on their decision making and who they are today. The suggested leadership activities serve as a stimulus to critical thinking and actions that make a difference for the young participants as well as their communities.

The final chapter illustrates the outcomes that can be expected by implementing the ideas and actions suggested by the chapters. We've included a section in this chapter called "Lessons Learned," to accommodate a colleague who reviewed an early draft and said everything was so positive that it didn't sound "real." Didn't we ever try something that didn't work? she asked. Oh, yes, we did! You will understand, by reviewing "Lessons Learned," that encouraging young people to give voice to the leader within has its challenges as well as its joys.

We are deeply indebted to the terrific young men and women who responded so passionately and frankly to our interviews, panel discussions, and e-mails. They represent an enchanting mix of rural and urban youth from a wide variety of cultures and faith traditions.

And while most of our examples are people we know personally, we're confident that, in some way, they also represent the young people our readers know, or will come to know, in their own good work. We're not the experts. Young people hold the truth when it comes to telling what works with youth. We can only share what we have learned through working with them. *Giving Voice to the Leader Within* is a practical application of what we've learned, experienced, and dreamed.

We want to thank the dynamic young people with whom we have served throughout our careers as well as our own families, who were the first to share our values, ideas, and actions. We learned from all of them along this exciting journey. They have challenged our thinking, invited us to grow with them, renewed our spirits, filled us with joy, and inspired us to continue leading.

Chapter One

Exploring Leadership

Taking the First Steps Together

Leaders come in all sizes, shapes, cultures, ethnicities, and genders. So do young people.

Leaders come from all walks of life. So do young people.

Leaders demonstrate their leadership in many different ways. So do young people.

Leaders make change happen. So do young people.

Leaders influence others. So do young people.

Is it any wonder that young people have the power and the potential to be leaders both now and in the future? In his essay on leadership development, John Gardner wrote, "Young people with substantial native gifts for leadership often fail to achieve what is in them to achieve. So part of our task is to develop what is naturally there but in need of cultivation."[1]

In other words, as parents and adults we have the wonderful opportunity to encourage young people to give voice to the leader within them. Doing so is challenging. It can be fun. It takes time and commitment. And it can be one of the most rewarding activities you will ever undertake. By connecting to

---

[1]John W. Gardner, "Leadership Development," Leadership Papers/7. Independent Sector, June 1987.

their world, we open the doors for young people to share with the world who they are—their ability to make a difference.

Can you imagine the thrill of seeing young people succeed, in part from what we've taught and shared with them and the challenges that we've set before them? You'll see our pride in young people as you trace their stories throughout this book.

For some young people, leadership is a natural capacity. They're captivated by a particular event or situation and become fired up to take action. They want to change the status quo. Or they have a passion for a particular cause or idea and, by sharing this passion, attract others to their cause. They are good at mobilizing both people and resources.

Their ongoing actions come as an expression of leadership that becomes a pattern for a value-centered life.

Because of their circumstances, natural attributes, experience, or relationships, they will emerge naturally as leaders. You often read about young people like these, especially in October when *USA Weekend,* in partnership with Points of Light Foundation, promotes "Make a Difference Day" across the country (www.makeadifferenceday.com).

But young people aren't just doing something in October. Their ongoing actions are an expression of leadership that becomes a pattern for a value-centered life.

For other young people, the power and the leadership potential are dormant; they simply haven't had the opportunities and space for their leadership to emerge. A few others have the passion and the power, but they use it for harm rather than for good. How can parents and caring adults provide opportunities for young people to access the power within them to express their leadership in positive, dynamic action?

Mike, one of the young people we interviewed for this book, said, "I believe that some people are natural-born leaders; others can obtain the skills necessary to lead; and others are more comfortable in supporting roles. The best thing to do is give all young people the opportunities to lead and provide them with support. It is then up to them to determine if they want to continue to seek out leadership roles." At age twenty-three, Mike is the chair of the board of directors of youthrive, a nonprofit organization founded in the fall of 2005. His preparation for this leadership position began when he was a high school student and served as co-chair of the Minnesota Alliance for Youth.

Like Mike's, our own experience suggests that a number of young people "practice" their leadership in supporting roles. They find joy in working behind the scenes with the knowledge that they can step into a more visible role if, and when, necessary.

The Millennials

Before we say too much more about young people and leadership, we need to take a few minutes to explore just who they are. Today's young people have been called the Y Generation or the Echo Boomers. Another name frequently given to them is the Millennials because they have grown up on either side of the millennium (born between 1982 and 1994) and been influenced by the events of that time.[2] In talking about their general characteristics, we also recognize that among the more than 60 million young people in this cohort, a number are disenfranchised and disengaged from our society. As in any group, there are individual differences and different situations. We want to keep all young people in mind, especially those who fall outside the general description that follows.

The Millennials have been described as the most protected generation in American history; in fact, their parents have been called "helicopter" parents because they are always "hovering" in the immediate area. These parents have organized nearly every moment of their children's lives—from play dates when they

---

[2]Lynne C. Lancaster and David Stillman, *When Generations Collide: Who They Are. Why They Clash. How to Solve the Generational Puzzle at Work* (New York: HarperBusiness, 2002); Ron Zemke, Claire Raines, and Bob Filipczak, *Generations at Work: Managing the Clash of Veterans, Boomers, Xers, and Nexters in Your Workplace* (New York: AMACOM, 2000).

were small, to sports, clubs, and lessons as they reached school age. Their parents have engaged them in decision making regarding family matters and told them to "speak up." As a result, the Millennials have grown up feeling very special and deserving of being treated accordingly. They feel especially close to their parents and talk to or e-mail them frequently.

For example, when Marlys conducted mock interviews with seniors at her alma mater prior to their first interviews with graduate school recruiters and prospective employers, she posed a situation and then asked, "What would you do in this situation?" The response she received from one of the candidates was, "Call my mom."

Technology—cell phones, computers, iPods, the Internet, video games, voice mail—are second nature to today's young people. They are used to finding information at the push of a button. Numerous articles in newspapers and magazines describe this phenomenon and the concerns experts have about it. Some say the use of personal technology is hurting some students academically and encouraging them to withdraw from society. Others say young people *are* connected to somebody—just in a different way than we usually think about it. While connecting through technology is a growing factor in today's society, we firmly believe that nothing works better than connecting in person, carrying out meaningful activities with young people across generations. It fosters strong relationships in places of the heart.

Today's young people have been also been exposed to corporate scandals, the terrorist attacks of September 11, 2001, the Iraq war, the explosion of the dot-com bubble, the Columbine school shootings, a declining economy, natural disasters, and the Oklahoma City bombing. Because they have been exposed to so much and are so diverse, they are also known as Global Citizens.

Millennials have grown up, for the most part, with a service ethic. Most of the organizations to which they belong carry out some type of community service project. They conduct food drives, clean up the environment, tutor younger children, visit nursing homes, and perform yard work and chores for elders in their communities. In all of these activities, young people are learning leadership skills and may, in fact, be in a position to become the newest generation to strongly commit to civic engagement and volunteering.

Knowing this about today's young people can help us connect with them in meaningful ways. Once they express an interest, we need to get them involved immediately or risk losing them. And we need to follow up. Too often adults make promises to young people but fail to follow through. Trust and respect are broken, and then we wonder why nothing gets done.

We need to see today's young people as the center of the experiences we are providing.

Young people are looking for ways to make their mark on society by participating in causes they believe in. In return, they expect and want us to believe in them.

We need to see today's young people as the center of the experiences we are providing. It's not about us and our need for them to be involved where we think they should be. Rather, we have to work around their interests and their availability, keeping their school and extracurricular commitments, their family priorities, and work obligations in mind. And we need to set meetings and events at their convenience, not ours.

In the beginning, the Minnesota Alliance with Youth,[3] a statewide organization that grew out of the President's Summit in 1997, met in the mornings. However, after many conversations about the importance of engaging young people, we rescheduled the meetings to late afternoons so that more of our youth could be involved. And Donna was always there to pick them up

---

[3]Marlys was the first co-chair of the Minnesota Alliance with Youth; Donna, its first director. Becky Jarvis was its first youth co-chair, and Maya Babu and Mike Radmer served as the second youth co-chairs. Jackie, Will Gaines, and Callie Tabor were all on the original steering committee of the Alliance.

at school or work and take them home when the meeting was over, using that special time for preparation and reflection.

For many adults, working with young people also means learning current technologies and new ways to communicate. To be effective we all need e-mail addresses—even instant messaging—and we need to feel comfortable using them. A great way to learn is to engage young people in teaching the technology to adults who are unfamiliar with "the territory."

The three of us have certainly benefited from our children's technological expertise, and the young experts who serve with us in various organizations love the "edge" that comes when they are the teacher!

Topics Explored

Giving Voice to the Leader Within explores how young people can express themselves as leaders and how caring adults can provide the *support, opportunities, space,* and *resources* for them to discover their leadership potential. Leadership can be learned. Adults can offer teachable moments to encourage young people to hear their inner call to step forward. They can encourage the setting of achievable goals that offer challenges and believe that young people can and will find their voice. These practical ideas can also be applied in working with natural leaders in search of opportunities

Adults need to be careful, however. Many of our interviewees suggested that teachers of leadership should not be forceful or authoritarian. "Let us figure it out on our own," they said. Young people also need to feel safe or comfortable enough in their relationship with adults to be able to express themselves effectively.

In the words of Merrill Associates:

The younger generation does not look for a Lone Ranger form of leadership. They don't believe that a larger-than-life individual can ride in, give direction, and lead the way to great accomplishments. They also do not view age, seniority and rank as measures of accomplishment or expertise. Unlike an earlier time when people admired their elders and followed them to victory, this generation does not see age as a dominant characteristic for leadership.[4]

Support

When we talk about caring adults giving support to young people to find that voice within, we mean engaging them in such a way as to build skills and practices for expressing their leadership potential. This engagement means listening attentively and then sharing our own values and experiences for creating change. It means encouraging them to create and tell their own stories, to mold and articulate their own values.

Another critical form of support comes when adults provide young people with the chance to demonstrate that "they can do it." Some young people don't believe they have a leadership voice until an adult encourages them by offering resources, support, and a shared commitment to a project or idea.

Authentic relationships are key. Adults need to be "real."

For example, a young man who was often suspended from school and demonstrated behavioral issues both in and out of class was invited by his teacher to be class leader for a specific project. His assignment was to represent the class in a presentation at a local museum. In preparing for the project, the teacher provided support and encouragement in this new role.

As a result, the student's presentation was a hit, and subsequently his grades and behavior improved. He saw himself in a leadership role; the appropriate behavior followed.

"You can teach all of this to others, but not in a seminar,"

---

[4]Merrill Associates, "Five Generational Differences Shaping leadership," Topic of the Month, August 2004 (www.merrillassociates.com).

said Mike. "It comes through human, person-to-person, interaction." Authentic relationships are key. Adults need to be "real."

Support is also about teaching critical thinking skills—going beyond providing youth entertainment, or token participation, or asking youth to follow a script written by an adult, or limiting youth engagement to performance groups. Telling young people what to think, what to say, and how to behave doesn't develop the coping mechanisms needed for real life. They need to experience and apply a variety of techniques to develop confidence in their ability to shape the future.

Opportunities

When we talk about caring adults creating opportunities for young people to find that voice within, we also mean involving them, authentically, in projects and on committees where they can create opportunities for self-expression and success that connect them, in positive ways, with the world around them. It means illustrating, by example, the interconnectedness and interdependence of our family and social systems. It also means being sensitive to young people's feelings.

For example, until he was seven, Via lived in a refugee camp in Thailand where everyone was Hmong. After coming to the United States, Via enrolled in a school where most of the children were Caucasian. This abrupt change in cultures, traditions, and language was quite a shock for Via. It made all the difference, however, in giving him an understanding of different ideas and perspectives. "I discovered," he said, "that despite the differences, we all had one thing in common, our feelings.

Young people need to be exposed to ways of lifestyle involving people other than their own race," said Via. "Exposure builds understanding," Via concluded.

What is most important is that adults offer options that broaden young people's understanding or discovery of what is possible.

Mike put it this way: "Adults can help by ensuring that opportunities for leadership and the practice of leadership are created so that when young people take over the world, they'll do a much better job."

Space

When we talk about caring adults giving space for young people to find that voice within, we mean encouraging young people to realize that life isn't all about "stuff."[5]

Providing this space means fostering young people's self-discovery about who they are and who they want to be and how they want to give of themselves to others. It involves helping them discover their own power, and then affirming it in positive ways.

According to Callie, co-creator of the "Connecting Is Key" campaign, youth accomplish great things, not by being smothered by adults, but by having the space to check out new concepts and theories on their own. "Once they initiate a thought," she said, "youth will follow it through with a little guidance from adults, especially if they are truly fascinated by the topic."

All youth, regardless of whether they are connected, over-connected, or not connected at all, need the space to be alone with themselves and their thoughts. For the highly scheduled Millennials, this can be a very difficult concept. Adults can be role models for the importance of personal time by living the connection between mind, body, and spirit. They can also build in time for reflection after activities (we provide suggestions at the end of each chapter).

Resources

When we talk about equipping young people with resources, we mean, for instance, offering transportation to meetings and providing meals or snacks when a project keeps everyone late. It

---

[5]Juliet B. Schor, *Born to Buy: The Commercialized Child and the New Consumer Culture* (New York: Scribner, 2004).

means sending invitations and providing scholarships or stipends for youth to participate in workshops or seminars. In other words, it means not only creating opportunities for them to share their knowledge and experience on community or conference panels, workshops, and forums, but also offering the resources they need to attend. It means accompanying them to meetings and events where they can meet people and build their own networks.

Resources may include sharing books, Web sites and articles—often spontaneously—as we come across them ourselves or by connecting young people with other adults who share a similar interest or who could make a difference in their lives. We can demonstrate the power of networking by inviting young people to meetings and introducing them to others in the room, pointing out a particular talent or attribute they bring to the gathering. Young people appreciate that we are thinking of them. They also appreciate that we find them valuable enough to share what we consider important and useful information. And they value the connections we foster that advance their education, careers, and leadership roles.

> *Interpersonal relationships and trust with young people are critical.*

Developing Relationships

Providing support, opportunities, space, and resources for young people takes energy and flexibility. It demands risk taking. It keeps us both humble and grateful. It requires patience, perseverance, vision, and, above all, caring. Finally, helping young people discover the voice within is all about relationships and trust.

In a world that is increasingly complex and impersonal, our ability to establish patterns of interpersonal relationships and trust with young people is critical. These relationships help them navigate the complexity of the world around them. The experiences we provide help them understand the myriad connections, partnerships, and relationships that are required to make our systems hum.

"Without support and motivation from a select group of

adults, my career as a leader may not have even begun," reports Callie. "It took the motivation of one single, open-minded adult to turn me into the leader I always wanted to be. This person demonstrated that leadership is all about trying new things and being creative ... sometimes all it may take is one person to say 'you can do this' to bring out that inner leader within us all. Youth are amazing in that they just need a little taste of success to spark something truly remarkable."

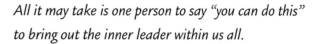

All it may take is one person to say "you can do this" to bring out the inner leader within us all.

After her first leadership experience, Callie went on to lead a statewide task force, create a youth partnership campaign, and serve as an adviser and keynote speaker for a national youth-related conference. Today Callie is finishing college and interning in a nonprofit with a focus on youth programs and leadership.

Visioning Leadership

If you are working with a group of young people on the topic of leadership, you may want to engage them in a discussion of several readings on leadership and then lead them in a series of activities that helps them create a vision of themselves as leaders, both now and in the future. Two of our favorite essays on the subject of leadership are "Essentials of Servant-Leadership," by Robert K. Greenleaf, and "What Makes a Leader," by Daniel Goleman;[6] however, many other worthy texts are also available for reading and exploring. Just select the ones that are meaningful for you and easy to assimilate.

During the discussions based on the texts you have assigned or suggested, you may want to ask questions like the following:

---

[6]Robert K. Greenleaf, "Essentials of Servant-Leadership," in Larry C. Spears and Michele Lawrence (eds.), *Focus on Leadership: Servant-Leadership for the 21st Century,* pages 19–26 (New York: John Wiley & Sons, 2002); Daniel Goleman, "What Makes a Leader?" *Harvard Business Review* November–December 1998, pages 93–102.

- How will you know if your leadership makes a difference?
- What do you see as the relationship between servant-leadership and EQ (emotional quotient)? Are they similar or different?
- How do these essays (or other texts) give you hope? Challenge you?
- What elements of our discussion can you take as part of your own life? What difference will it make if you incorporate them?

After a large-group discussion, you can divide the group into smaller groups for young people to consider who they think exemplifies the leadership attributes you've discussed or how the leaders that they know exemplify either servant-leadership or EQ. Each small group can report the outstanding examples they've identified.

This process of reading, discussing, and identifying can be a great springboard for young people to do a visioning activity about the spirit or leadership potential that resides in each of them. When conducted in a relaxed, trustful, and nonthreatening environment, visioning can help young people dream their future and cast themselves as the individuals they want to become.

To start the visioning, encourage young people to visualize or draw pictures or words that represent leadership to them. (You can even have an assortment of magazines for them to page through for ideas.) By doing so, they will be generating a visual image of their own leadership potential. When the pictures or words are clearly in front of them, either on paper or in their minds, ask group members, first, to visualize themselves as leaders in their community and, second, to visualize the changes that occur in their community because of their leadership. Begin by asking them to close their eyes while you guide their vision by suggesting that they imagine themselves in their community, what they are doing as leaders, what issues they are facing, how they are responding to the issues, who else is involved, what the potential solutions might be, and so forth. Use statements that stimulate their imagined scenes and give life to their ideas.

After you've given them time to create a visual image, invite group members to come back to the present; ask each person who wishes to do so to share her or his leadership vision. Sharing is an opportunity for each to articulate and make real the direction or focus they seek for themselves.

To take it even deeper, you might also ask the whole group, or again divide into smaller groups, to explore what might help them reach their leadership visions.

By visioning their future as leaders, young people have the opportunity to dream, get in touch with themselves, and establish a creative focus or direction that will guide them throughout their lives.

Tasks of Leadership

Many writers and practitioners have defined the tasks of leadership. According to Peter Drucker, the acknowledged father of modern management, the only common element of leaders is that they all have followers. He believes that because leaders are visible, they must set an example, focus on results, and take responsibility for what happens.[7]

Recognizing the leader within ourselves as adults is the first task for us in encouraging young people to find their own leadership voice. "We can tell when adults have confidence," said Paul, a student leader from St. Peter, Minnesota. "In teachers you can tell the minute they walk into the room. They need leadership within themselves, first, before they can inspire us."

Once we adults are comfortable with and understand our own style of leadership, we can take the responsibility to develop it in others. As adults, we set an example by our own behavior and

---

[7]Peter Drucker, "Foreword," in Frances Hesselbein, Marshall Goldsmith, and Richard Beckhard (eds.), *The Leader of the Future: New Visions, Strategies and Practices for the Next Era,* page xii (San Francisco: Jossey-Bass, 1996).

values. We stand as positive symbols of what can be done when we invest our own energy and passion in leading our families, organizations, communities, and nation.

This vitality and energy attracts others, especially young people, when it includes a role for them. Maya says, "Adults who take the time to really know a young person are the ones who help us grow into leaders."

Young people can tell when adults are passionate about something. "You can tell which ones really care about kids," said Kristi. Our panel of high school students also talked about how much they love it when their teachers are passionate about the subject they teach. "Can you imagine," they asked, "being passionate about rocks?"

It happens. The passion shows. It draws others into the experience. Adults can ignite this passion for young people to create leadership experiences. As one of their projects, students in Marlys's Gustavus Adolphus College interim course in nonprofit management visited and interviewed leaders at a wide range of nonprofit organizations. The students discovered a common thread among them: passion for mission!

"My passion for wanting to help others was fueled even more by the rewards pointed out for both me and those I'd help," reflected one student. "Seeing the passion in people who have been doing this type of work for twenty to thirty years makes me stronger in my desire to work for a nonprofit," she added.

By sharing our passions and demonstrating that we, as adults, care about what happens, we provide ongoing, teachable moments for leadership. By engaging young people in a broad array of experiences, we are creating and fostering the motivation for lives of service. "I admire adults who see youth not as young and inexperienced," said Callie, "but as a source of new ideas and a fresh outlook."

As adults, we also need to give ourselves space—space to listen to our own voice as well as to the voices of young people, space to reflect, to focus, to be more attentive, and to be in touch with our own voice within. This allows us to express the spirit and disciplines of true leadership: flexibility, openness, acceptance, listening, respect, empathy, passion, compassion, and encouragement, to name a few qualities.

Central to giving ourselves space is also relinquishing the need to be in control, the need to be recognized as the expert. And this is so hard to do! We need to let go of past methods of doing things and embrace change—to model being open to risk taking, even when the possibility is failure. As one of our young people said, "Through failure, we learn."

By being open-minded, we can see the best in each young person, build on it, and nurture it. We can also demonstrate our willingness to be true partners—to be open to the fact that we don't know it all—and willing to say, "Let's find out together."

Why is all of this important? Because our future (theirs, too) depends on it. We need to inspire and pass on our passions and interest in service as integral to a successful and meaningful life. If we fail, we are faced with the lost potential of each young person. We also fail to foster a new generation of leaders ready to effect positive change.

If we see the potential in each young person and provide *support, opportunities, space,* and *resources,* we present them with an incredible, challenging "high"—their potential for making a difference realized.

Reflections—Your Thoughts and Inspirations

Taking time to reflect on our experiences deepens our learning. It fosters critical thinking and analysis. Use the following suggestions to gain new insight into your own experiences, articulate them in writing, and apply that awareness to connect more effectively with young people.

1. Think about your leadership experiences as a young person or adult. How were they positively influenced, supported, and encouraged by the adults around you? How can you replicate any of these experiences for the youth around you today?

_____

_____

_____

_____

_____

2. What experiences made you the leader you are today? Are these same experiences available to young people now? How do today's opportunities differ? What opportunities can you create within your sphere of influence?

_____

_____

_____

_____

_____

3. How do you stand as a "positive example" of what leaders can be?

_____

_____

_____

_____

_____

4. What are you doing to create space for yourself? How do you focus so that you have time for thinking and renewing?

_____

_____

_____

_____

_____

5. What are the barriers to leadership for young people where you live? How might they be overcome or circumvented? What's your role in the process?

_____

_____

_____

_____

_____

Leadership Activities—Your Actions

For each of the activities described below, determine what specific steps you will take to complete the activity, a timeline for doing so, and a statement or two about what you hope to accomplish by completing the activity. Finally, indicate what resources you'll need to make it happen.

1. List the organizations in which you are involved. What leadership opportunities exist for young people in these organizations? Invite several young people to join you and then provide the support and space they need for successful learning experiences.

_____

Action Steps:

_____

Timeline:

Desired Outcomes:

Resources:

2. Identify one young person that you believe has leadership potential. Ask her or him to join you in a shared experience such as a city council meeting, conference, or networking event. Be the motivator, the encourager, the connector, the networker, the skill builder for this young person. Increase the options. Increase the experiences. Increase the exposure.

Action Steps:

Timeline:

Desired Outcomes:

Resources:

3. Adults often need encouragement to be open and to reach out to youth. Identify an adult friend or colleague with whom you can discuss youth leadership. Offer to work in partnership with her or him or serve as a your friend's mentor as he or she establishes a relationship with a young leader. Share this book (or buy your friend a copy as a gift) and help your friend get started in encouraging young people to give voice to the leader within.

Action Steps:

Timeline:

Desired Outcomes:

Resources:

4. Connect with your high school principal or district superintendent or with the leader of a youth group in your community or congregation. Explore how you and like-minded adults might connect with and coach or mentor young people who are ready for leadership experiences.

Action Steps:

Timeline:

Desired Outcomes:

Resources:

---

5. Convene a group of young people to explore what they consider to be tasks of leadership. Based on the conversation, work with them to create an action plan that allows greater opportunities and space for growing their leadership. Be the supportive adult who helps them carry out the plan and connects them to the resources that can make it happen.

Action Steps:

Timeline:

Desired Outcomes:

Resources:

Actions—Your Afterthoughts

After you've carried out each activity or its modification, reflect on the experience using the following guide.

1. What happened when I tried this?

_____

_____

_____

2. What did I learn?

_____

_____

_____

3. What changes will I make the next time I try it?

_____

_____

_____

4. How did these actions help young people give voice to the leader within?

_____

_____

_____

Chapter Two

Support

Being the Wind beneath Their Wings

In order for many young people to give voice to the leader within, they need the support and guidance of parents and caring adults who are willing to go beyond providing entertainment or telling them what to think and do. These significant adults offer support by helping young people gain confidence in their ability to make good decisions, take action, and affect change.

Demonstrating support involves more than saying the right words. It also demands action. And it demands a belief that young people have both the ability and the talent to be leaders, that their voice is as important and valuable as the adult voice. "Just believing in a young person is essential and can be a motivating force," said Michael. "If you believe in me, I'm going to believe in myself. There is a self-affirming process in that belief. It's not through words, but actions."

As adults, we offer support best when we see youth as resources, seek their ideas and opinions, and engage them in authentic activities that utilize their talents, attributes, and skills. Young people know when we are genuine.

Motivation

While believing in young people can be a motivating force, we were surprised by the number of young people who said that self-motivation was also key to becoming a leader. "You must," said Paul, "have that desire to improve, to be better." A lot of times this internal motivation is to achieve a particular goal (for example, in sports or in the classroom), but it can be more.

Michael was expelled from school in seventh grade and arrested for spraying Mace in the halls of his school. His mom left him in jail overnight. When she picked him up, she said, "I've tried my best. From now on your life is in your hands, and you can do whatever you want with it." Michael knew he had to find a way back.

As adults, we offer support best when we see youth as resources.

"That was the most important turning point in my life—giving me control of my life," said Michael. "I had the whole summer to think about it and decide where I was going. I knew I had to change. So that summer I rode my bike from school to school, trying to find one that would accept me. Finally, the principal at Brooklyn Center [Minnesota] High School gave me a paper for my mom to sign and followed it up with a conference. I was in!"

Michael's inner motivation earned him a second chance. Through his own perseverance, he found someone who was willing to support his decision to get back into school and engage him in a way to take advantage of this determination. "I have this sense that there is something else to be done," he said. "It drives me. It's physical. I can feel it."

Michael's self-motivation was critical. Combined with the support and encouragement of a very special English teacher, his life turned around. She suggested that he run for student council or class president, a capacity in which he would automatically sit on the student council. He was successful in his bid for election and went on to serve for four consecutive years.

Today Michael is a political science and international management major at Hamline University in St. Paul, Minnesota, an Alan Page scholarship recipient, and the recipient of the Presidential Service Award for the 2003 design, implementation, and success of the Fast Forward project.

Fast Forward, first introduced to the Brooklyn Center schools, matches qualified and committed high school seniors with seventh- and eighth-grade students who have failed, or are at risk of failing, an entire grade level. The seniors meet with middle school students two or three times each week for one semester to help improve academic success and build ongoing friendships.

Thomas, the seventh grader paired with Michael, went from having failed a grade level (repeating seventh grade) with straight F's to a B average in just one semester. Interviewed by KARE 11 (a Minneapolis, Minnesota, TV station) News, Thomas said of Michael, "He told me one time to achieve greatness, you have to give up something. So he helped me get rid of some of my distractions and helped me get on the right track."

"You often have to change yourself to get what you want," reported Kristi, one of the St. Peter students. "You may need to develop new skills and knowledge."

Adults and young people in leadership positions can provide the experiences in which students discover and get in touch with their own motivations and passions.

Ways to Create Support

Skill Building

Writing, speaking, and other communication skills are critical assets for every leader. So, how do we build these skills in young people? First, start with a small group and position them to write and speak about an issue or activity. Next, review with them what they have written and prepared and offer positive suggestions for change or emphasis prior to their engagement. The old axiom rings true: practice makes perfect. Thorough preparation increases a young person's chance of success.

For example, each year young people are invited to serve as emcees and keynote speakers at Search Institute's Healthy Communities • Healthy Youth Conference. (Search Institute is a national nonprofit organization, headquartered in Minneapolis,

Minnesota. Its mission is to provide leadership, knowledge, and resources to promote healthy children, youth, and communities.) This means addressing approximately 1,500 people, a daunting task even for adults.

In preparing for the 2002 conference, Donna, the youth engagement coordinator, first worked with Willie, Callie, Via, and Erko by practicing, in private, major points that they wanted to emphasize in their presentations. They reviewed a prewritten script to identify key points and then put the main points into their own words to make the presentations flow more easily and express their own personalities.

The students then moved to the stage and practiced in front of their peers. After each practice session, they reflected on their performance and received lots of encouragement. By the time the conference arrived, they each presented beautifully and confidently.

Equal in importance to the practice was the friendly face or two in the front row, both before and during the presentation, offering smiles and nods of encouragement. We all need affirmation. Be there. Be present at pivotal times in young people's lives.

Another activity that builds critical skills is teaching or tutoring others. "I learned that when I was teaching kids, I was learning the most," Michael reported. "You can't be hypocritical; you have to learn it, believe in it, and live it. It's all intertwined."

The development of coping skills is also critical for young people. They need to know how to work through life's challenges, and they need support in developing coping mechanisms to use when things don't go right. Samantha said that when her mother was diagnosed with cancer, she began to recognize what was really important in life. This recognition and focus helped her see things in a new way and affected her leadership experiences.

The young people in St. Peter related to a different style of coping. They told us about a teacher who allowed retakes on tests in their advanced placement chemistry class. "You're capable of getting a better score," he'd said, but would leave the decision to retake the test up to them. If students wanted a second try, he would go over the entire test with them before providing a new, harder exam that covered the same material. One of the group reported that in retaking the exam, his score increased from 53 to 100! The group, as a whole, felt that the teacher's demonstration of his belief in them raised their confidence level. As you can see from this example, young people benefit from opportunities for a second chance. The "redo" reinforces their learning.

On the concept level, many young people know they have the power to lead. We simply need to provide them the opportunities to demonstrate that they "can do it." Involvement in a project from the planning stages forward to implementation and evaluation is a case in point.

As adults, we also need to keep in mind that the true outcome is not the success of a particular event, but rather the experience of putting it together. When things don't go as planned, you use the experience as a "teachable" moment and reflect on what could be done differently another time. As the young people are figuring it out, we can support their discussions and actions.

Critical Thinking Skills

While the Millennials are probably the best-informed generation in American history, one of the criticisms of the group is that they want information packaged for their consumption and aren't interested in taking the time to methodically work through problems and issues.

Therefore, the more experiences and options we can provide that strengthen young people's skills and desire to dig "deeper and broader," the better. While planning activities with them, we can explore their intended outcomes and determine how those outcomes can be measured and evaluated.

While exposing young people to various options, adults can also explore with them a process for analyzing the opportunities/ challenges of the options, or the benefits/costs. This process is helpful for arriving at the best choice and is a method that can be used by young people throughout their lives. They learn to examine both the positive results and the negative implications of a situation in terms of dollars, time, people power, knowledge, and so forth.

Because the Millennials are so culturally diverse compared to previous generations, asking students to reframe questions or scenarios from their various points of view and in different words can be very revealing and lead to healthy discussions. Likewise, gathering information from various sources to inform the group prior to taking action allows students to synthesize the material and look for common ground.

The young people planning the 2004 Healthy Communities • Healthy Youth Conference identified war as their number one issue. This engendered a long discussion of the definitions of war and peace. They then explored what could be done to promote peace on different levels: personally, in their communities, in society, and globally.

Along the way, they also explored the sources of the information they gathered to inform their discussion and how those sources might have been influenced. Were they from a conservative Web site or talk show? A liberal one? Did the source impact the content?

These types of discussions requiring critical thinking can be generated on just about any topic young people find of interest. Our goal is to raise thinkers and informed change agents with ethical decision-making skills!

Another great technique for building critical thinking skills is to role play. When youth associated with the Youth Department of the Walnut Avenue Women's Center in Santa Cruz, California, wanted to plan a "battle of the bands," the facilitators resisted telling them what they might miss in the planning. Instead, they created scenarios that would "reveal" the missing elements. For example, one of the facilitators pretended to be a youth at the event who cut himself and asked for help. This "revealed" the need for first-aid. Another came forward to report that a huge gang fight was brewing outside the gym. This "revealed" the need for security.

With another group planning an outing, this same organization role-played questions like, "Who wants to sit next to me in the car?" This question "revealed" the need for transportation for the activity.

Active Listening

Adults serve as great role models as well as supporters when they demonstrate active listening. By engaging young people in life conversations and acting as sounding boards for their ideas, we affirm their value. When we truly listen—before offering our own advice and ideas—we demonstrate that we care about them and their opinions.

As Samantha said, "Adults need to relate to you; be a listener; generate ideas with you; add to your ability to have a variety of perspectives."

As part of this listening dialogue, we can learn about the aspirations and dreams of young people. We can suggest alternative actions, explore various options, and ask, "What can I do to help you reach your desired goal?"

How do you know if you are really an active listener?

- Do you give the speaker your full, nonjudgmental attention?
- Do you think about what you are hearing—not what you are going to say in response?
- Do you ask questions to clarify meaning or feelings?
- Do you listen for main ideas?
- Do you refrain from interrupting with your own story no matter how relevant it might be?
- Do you examine ideas by mentally summarizing and outlining key points?
- Do you focus on what the speaker is saying rather than anticipating what he might say?

- Do you respond positively thus sending the message that you are listening carefully?

Using the above suggestions, practice actively listening with a young person. Take turns listening to each other and then offering feedback. Did the speaker feel respected? Listened to? How could the listener have been more effective? Practice makes perfect for adults as well as for young people.

Storytelling

Teaching young people how to tell stories is a sure-fire way to increase their ability to attract others to their cause or to demonstrate a particular issue. It's also a great way to build relationships among the generations.

For example, a three-generation family gathers every summer. The practice grew out of the discovery that parents and grandparents "went nuts" at Christmas, resulting in an overflow of gifts that lost their meaning and significance. "What would you think," asked the grandmother, "if we traded the excess at Christmas for a family vacation?" Thus a new tradition was born and, with it, a new way to discover the joys of intergenerational storytelling.

At its annual gathering, the family posts a number of questions and statements. For example, "Think back to the last three birthdays. Do you remember what you received as presents? What was the one that meant the most to you?" Or, "Think about a time when you were lost. How did you feel? How did you become 'unlost'? What did you learn from the experience?"

Each family member is invited to select the question or statement of her or his choice. On the designated evening, the family forms a circle of sorts, and each person tells a story based on her or his selection. Many questions and statements are possible. Ahead of the gathering, you can even poll family members for ideas. This kind of participation draws them into the activity from the beginning and enhances the fun.

The resulting stories are poignant, funny, and oftentimes revealing of the family member's inner self. The family has drawn closer because of the stories, and shy family members have grown more articulate in expressing themselves in a group. Believe us when we say that the activity—and the stories that are shared—will be ones family members will remember the rest of their lives. In fact, each year's activity is frequently preceded by a recount of one or two stories that have come before.

This technique can be used as an icebreaker for groups of young people as well as for adults. It can be used as a starting activity for a discussion on how storytelling enhances leadership and the ability to persuade. The discussion might be prompted by asking for feedback on the storytelling. What stories elicited the most passionate response? Did gestures play a part? Did the attitude of the storyteller make a difference? And so forth.

Another great idea to build storytelling skills is to gather youth into small groups and introduce an activity called "Story in a Box," the brainchild of communications specialist Pat Whitney.

Story in a Box

Prior to the gathering, put six to ten objects in a box. When the group is convened, divide into three subgroups and pass the box among them, allowing each subgroup to examine the box and its contents thoroughly before passing it to the next. Allow ten to fifteen minutes for the subgroups to create a particular part of a story based on the contents of the box. For example, instruct the first subgroup to create the setting for the story, the second to create the plot, and the third to create a plausible ending.

The stories can be general in nature, or the facilitator can suggest that the story be related to a particular organization, incident, or issue.

Once the allotted time is over, call on the first subgroup to present the setting. Then, invite the second subgroup to expand on the story with the plot it designed, and finally, ask the third subgroup to conclude the story. Not only does the activity demand cooperation, logical thought, and creativity, it also generates howls of laughter. In a really large group, a variety of boxes can be created so that an assortment of stories emerges and everyone can be involved.

Storytelling also increases the ability to listen; it engenders trust as we take into consideration the storyteller's ideas and feelings, and it stimulates a sense of community by all who share in the stories that are told and the passions that are revealed. Additionally, the storyteller feels valued and listened to.

Building Daily Practices

We support young people through our daily practices. Parents set the stage when they actively live out their values and practices, and their children are most likely to reflect those same practices and values throughout their own adulthood. For example, young people who volunteer with their parents as youngsters are more likely to volunteer as adults. Seeing service as a necessary part of life builds confidence and the importance of contributing.

In south Minneapolis, Minnesota, Haley (seven) and Jack (four) lived next door to an elderly woman named Mildred. Their dad mowed Mildred's yard in the summer and shoveled her walks in the winter. The children were encouraged by their parents to draw pictures for Mildred and leave them in her mailbox, and they helped their mom make cookies for her on a regular basis. One warm summer day, their regular neighborly practice turned into something more. Called by Mildred's niece, who hadn't been able to reach her aunt by phone for two days, the family went over to assess the situation. Receiving no response to their insistent pounding on the door, Haley and Jack's dad was able to raise a small window next to the air conditioner.

The space was just large enough for Haley to slip through. Her instructions were to go immediately to the front door and open it for her parents.

As she walked through the house to the front door, Haley nearly tripped over Mildred, who had fallen, broken her hip, and was unable to move. Once Haley opened the door, her parents immediately called 911. Luckily,

Mildred recovered and subsequently moved to a nursing home. The family now lives several hours away, yet they continue sending cards and pictures drawn by the children. They also set aside a day every few months to visit her.

The daily practice of caring for their neighbor has left a lasting impression on Haley and Jack. They know the importance of service to others. They know their action made a difference in Mildred's life. Their parents continue to model this ethic and join with the children in a variety of community and school projects.

Small, local environments often allow children and young people safe opportunities to demonstrate that they can lead, that they can make a difference. We support their efforts by engaging them in the systems and processes of our communities and by introducing them to the connections and relationships among various community groups. As one of the young people we interviewed exclaimed, "Leadership can be as simple as helping someone cross the street. We don't have to be CEOs."

Kindling the Spirit for Leadership

Helping young people trust their own intuitions, sometimes in spite of logic, fosters creativity and confidence. According to Erko, one of our interviewees, "You can't teach confidence, but you can give someone the opportunity to gain it." "Confidence," said Will, "gives youth the ability to pursue more and more skills. It opens a door that leads to endless possibilities of knowledge."

Interest in the spirit for leadership often comes at an early age. After a memorial for a great-grandparent, a family was gathered around a fire pit in the back yard. Alex, a preschooler, said, "Wait everyone. I'm going to get sticks."

> *"You can't teach confidence, but you can give someone the opportunity to gain it."*

While the adults scratched their heads in wonder, Alex gathered up sticks in the yard and passed them among the group. "Light them on fire," he requested. "Light them for Grandma Ruth." When everyone had followed his lead, Alex said, "Now we're going to say something about her."

"Do you want us to say it out loud?" his mother asked.

"No," Alex responded. "Say it in your head."

Silence followed. After a few minutes Alex said, "Now throw your sticks in the fire and let her spirit go."

The family was dumbfounded at what they had heard and seen. They talked about it for weeks. Alex heard what everyone said about what he had done and was affirmed by their remarks. The family's reaction will encourage similar behavior in the future. By being observant and tuned in to young people, we can reinforce their spirit. We can say, "I liked how you . . ." or "I just noticed that . . ." with joy in our voices.

Donna describes a person's spirit as who you are at your core—how you fill a room with energy. Your spirit comes through in your interactions with others. Some people are said to have a peaceful spirit, others a strong spirit, others a genuine spirit, and so forth.

Kyle is known in his family and among his peers as a "calming" spirit because he seems to have a calming effect on a room. He listens intensely. His spirit comes through when he shares and becomes part of the environment around him. Kyle's mom says that adults' response to him builds on this spirit. She believes he developed this spirit of patience and empathy when she had twins, and he became responsible for helping her with the babies.

"The more new things young people learn," she says, "the more responsibility they have to use it, model it, teach it, and share it in some way."

In addition to kindling the spirit of leadership and supporting its expression, we need to encourage young people to find or make time for feeding their own spirit—time to think and reflect, and time to be silent. Taking care of oneself brings balance to life. One needs to be renewed in order to continue giving and leading.

Recognition and Respect

Just as Alex was recognized for his spirit and behavior by his family, young people need and want recognition, especially from their peers, but also from people they respect and whom they consider leaders.

Sometimes recognition comes simply in the form of a thank-you. All of the young people we interviewed talked about the importance of being appreciated. They suggested using comments like the following: "Thanks for taking on that responsibility." "Thanks for your effort in bringing people together." "Thanks for your time." "I really value your thinking on this issue." Eric concluded our discussion by saying, "When people compliment you, you feel better inside. It reinforces what you are doing."

Marlys regularly cuts and mails articles to the students from her church who are highlighted in the local newspaper. The mom of one of the recipients mentioned to Marlys how much it meant to her daughter. "It wasn't about the recognition," she said. "It was that you *noticed*." If this is true for a student who is already recognized in the media, think how much more important it is for young people who don't receive this attention.

Recognition by those whom they regard as leaders, as well as by their peers, means a lot. "When you look up to someone—and they turn around and see you as a leader, as a positive role model—that is the best recognition," reported Kristi. "How adults reinforce particular qualities in you is important, but recognition by peers is more important than anything else. Having them acknowledge you is critical."

Knowing the Millennials' penchant for technology, the use of e-mails, pictures, and phone messages are effective vehicles for expressing your appreciation for their contributions.

Adults need to be careful, though, our students said, in "over recognition." When one person gets too much credit, jealousy can rear its ugly head. This can be overcome if we also teach our young people when and how to share the credit by recognizing others who may have contributed to their success.

Donna is always on the lookout for little mementos and tokens that might be used as reminders of the success or interests of the young people with whom she is connected. When she presents the appropriate gift, the young person can recall the memory of how he or she was successful as well as the feeling that went with the experience. This kind of acknowledgment also helps young people realize the importance of gratitude and validates different forms of leadership, such as involvement behind the scene.

For example, when she was in Washington, D.C., Donna brought home books about the various American presidents for Will and Callie, co-creators of "Connecting Is Key," because she knew of their special interest in the presidency. The gifts both strengthened their relationship and reinforced the value of their relationship. Presenting Will and Callie with a gift demonstrated that Donna knew the young people as individuals and respected their interests beyond the specific project that they were working on together.

Being in young people's lives, outside of the specific activities you might share, expands who we are and our understanding of the world. When we attend their school events, concerts, games, and life milestones, we experience the thrill of being in their lives. Let's commit to making the focus of our relationship with young people the whole person.

Values

Deciding on the most important aspects in life can help young people put things in perspective, especially when they have difficult choices to make. Do they value power, truth, happiness, honor, obedience, integrity, peace, loyalty, fairness, excellence, learning, adventure, spirituality, success, humor, teamwork, service, relationships, wisdom?

Depending upon a young person's culture, experience, family, and community connections, a variety of other values might be included on this list.

We support young people by actively living our own values and our passions. This requires focus and an ability to be strong, to be committed. Young people do take notice when we match our words with our actions. It's the old adage remade: "Do as I say and do as I do."

"You can tell which student teachers are going to make it," said one panel of teens we interviewed. "They are the ones that have an enthusiasm, a spark, an 'I want to be here' attitude." Hannah laughed and observed, "You can immediately tell how well you can manipulate them by the way they walk into the room. If they come in looking like they know what they are talking about, you won't get away with anything. You can tell if they are passionate about being a teacher—and their subject matter. They not only tell it like it is, they follow through."

> *Young people do take notice when we match our words with our actions.*

Think about how a car acts when the wheels are out of alignment. It's hard to keep it going straight on the road; it's wobbly. The same thing happens when we behave in a manner not congruent with our values and our passions. In fact, that's exactly when values can get us into trouble—when there is a gap between what we say and what we do. In other words, "we need to put our money where our mouth is!"

Leaders stand for something, demonstrate integrity, and have the courage of their convictions. They also create an environment that models the values they wish to nurture. By knowing what we stand for, we can guide young people in discovering the values in their own lives.

We need to be watching and provide support for the choices that they make—even when those choices might be different from our own. We can be regular sounding boards for young people who need someone to challenge or help interpret their ideas and values.

Many of the young people whom we interviewed talked about the importance of values they learned at home. According to Maya, "The home inspires a commitment to other people and an understanding that you are part of a broader community." Mike agreed. "When we are young," he said, "we learn initially by copying. We learn our values by what happens at home."

When young people don't learn positive values at home, we need to expose them to the possibilities. For example, one of the young men in a youth group struggled with the responsibility of being someplace on time. He had no concept of the use of an alarm clock to get up in the morning and to be on time because no one in his home had ever used an alarm clock. The adult leader used the situation as a personal, teachable moment and an opportunity to present a small gift in a way, and in a place, that respected his sensitivity and illustrated his value to the group.

It helps young people to verbalize the values they've learned by stating, "This is what I do." "This is what I stand for." Putting values in concrete terms is a powerful tool when faced with a difficult choice. When young people know who they are and what they stand for, their personal performance is increased, and they feel good about what they do. Being able to articulate their values and their passions helps young people figure out what to do without having to ask for guidance.

A middle school student considered herself a follower until her teacher, Anne Parish, placed her in a leadership role in a service-learning class. This student-driven class, supported by the teacher, focuses on teen issues such as school violence, media influence on teen behavior, racism, and substance abuse. The young woman, encouraged in her role as a leader, bravely stood up for herself and promoted healthy choices by her schoolmates. Now she and her entire class have accepted a leadership role in the school; they hold schoolwide forums once a week in morning assemblies to present, discuss, and find solutions to issues faced by teens.

When asked, "How do you know when a situation will have positive results?" Michael said, "Sometimes when I have to make a decision, I don't always go with the first thing that comes along. There's something inside me that says to wait before making a decision. It's inside—some of it is my value system."

The root word for values is the same one for valor. This comes from the Latin *valere,* meaning "to be strong." To be strong in our convictions and strong in our ability to transmit those convictions is a mark of positive leadership.

Young people find many ways to express their values—by saying no to negative opportunities; by stepping out in front, often alone, to rally others around a cause; and by simply doing something kind for another human being. For example, they can stand up for someone who is being put down by making positive comments to counteract the negative ones. In other words, values and actions are usually congruent. They are aligned.

Personal values are powerful signposts on the road to giving voice to the leader within. Remember the oft-repeated line, "If you don't know where you are going, you might end up someplace else"? Being clear about our values reveals who we are as leaders. One can say, for example, that key individuals in gangs are leaders. It's their values that are different.

"There are two different types of leaders," said Jamie, "good and bad." Even if people don't have good values, they can be leaders. They choose to express their passion in a negative form. The young people in one of our focus groups agreed that it was up to them—not their parents, teachers, or other adults—to use their passion, spirit, and values in a positive manner.

As leaders, young people can set standards and be an example in their personal lives, and in their schools, organizations, and communities. By being true to their values, they can define what is to be done, shape the process for action, train others, communicate how it is to be done, and celebrate what has been accomplished. "My most valuable skill," said Will, "my golden ticket, is knowing how to work with people. Happiness is ensured for everyone who can work with anyone."

Change, and the complex systems and organizations in which we live, often challenge our values. We can support young people in their struggle to adapt to change by illustrating ways to weigh and balance what are often competing values or to consider alternative actions. In doing so, we develop critical thinkers.

The Declaration of Independence reads, "We hold these truths to be self-evident," yet the courts continue to interpret what this means on a regular basis. In like manner, we are helping young people interpret their values by expanding their options and opportunities in the decision-making process.

Sometimes, however, young people, as well as adults, can find themselves in situations where their values are not congruent with the organization or activity in which they are involved. What happens then? People have a number of options: they can accept what is and integrate the new values into their own; they can try to change the values or the expression of the values in the situation; they can ride it out—go along with the crowd; or they can excuse themselves and move on.

These types of decisions can be agonizing for young people. Situations are seldom black and white—rather they are grayer in color. Nor are many situations a simple matter of right or wrong. Often the choices can be between two "rights." Another issue at stake in situations like these is the reconciliation of our need to be "good" and to feel important.

A number of young people felt undervalued when working with an adult leader with an authoritarian style. They felt she wasn't listening to what they had to say, that she gave lip service only, and that she had a condescending attitude.

They got together and talked about staging a protest. After reviewing this option, they realized that they really couldn't change the adult leader. When someone suggested that they should accept the situation for the greater good, a number of them said they couldn't handle it. They chose to leave the organization.

When young people don't show up, it is almost always because they don't see an active role for themselves. Their value for inclusion is missing. Once they leave, it's nearly impossible to get them to return. As adults, we must take a look at our style and the relationship between the values we espouse and the actions we take. Relating to a young person as a whole—in an authentic, honest, and respectful manner—creates a supportive environment in which a young person thrives.

The young people who left the group with the authoritarian leader acted with the support of a caring adult who provided the emotional support and space for the young people to select the option that was best for them in the circumstances. The supportive adult encouraged them to weigh the situation and the potential consequences. He challenged them to think deeply about the decisions they were about to make. Once decisions were made, he affirmed the choice, offered constructive feedback, and stepped back!

While much has been written about leadership attributes, we note that values head the list of the following attributes that have been important in our own lives.

Leaders

- Know and express their values.
- Share their passion and invite others to join them, create a team, and a plan for action.
- Locate and gather resources to support the plan.
- Exercise critical thinking skills that lead to ethical decisions.
- Create balance in their lives and set aside time for renewal.
- Turn failures into learning and celebrate positive outcomes.
- Express gratitude and show appreciation for everyone's contribution.
- Are open to new opportunities and willing to take positive risks.

Positive Energy

Leadership springs from a dynamic network of committed people. By creating positive energy and modeling values, we attract young people. By offering them experiences to live their values, we contribute to their growth as leaders. Keep in mind Will's observation that it is infinitely more valuable to let a youth see a faulty idea through to the end than for the youth to watch an adult's idea reach success. "The latter will do plenty for your confidence," he said, "but nothing for the youth." However, we can answer questions along the way to help young people clarify their options and engage in critical thinking.

> *By offering them experiences to live their values, we contribute to their growth as leaders.*

At the same time, we must be mindful never to put a young person out on a limb alone. If the limb is chopped off, a supportive adult needs to be on hand to engage the young person in reflection so that the experience can be mined for constructive learning and the young person can feel valued and grow in confidence.

Support for young people to find and express the leader within comes in many forms. Basic to all is acceptance of them, as they are, and the commitment to listen, really listen, to what they have to offer. Just by having an adult listen to what they have to say, youth often arrive at their own solutions. This builds confidence in their own abilities as well as trust in the adult.

Reflections—Your Thoughts and Inspirations

Taking time to reflect on our experiences deepens our learning. It fosters critical thinking and analysis. Use the following suggestions to gain new insight into your own experiences, articulate them in writing, and apply that awareness to connect more effectively with young people.

1. Think about the values that exemplify you. Where did they come from? How did they become integrated into your personal value system? Name two ways you can use this knowledge to connect with young people.

_____

_____

_____

_____

_____

2. Ethics are about moral courage. When was the last time you stood up for and spoke out on something you thought was right, not necessarily what was popular? What happened as a result?

_____

_____

_____

_____

_____

3. When was the last time you received recognition for something you did? How did it make you feel? How can you offer others recognition for their contributions? What mementos can you give the young people who are close to you that fit their interests/accomplishments?

_____

_____

_____

_____

_____

4. How do you feed and renew your spirit? When do you feel in a state of calm, peace? Do you use specific techniques? Readings? Music? Mental imagery? How do you share your spirit? Who are the people that add to your energy and enthusiasm?

_____

_____

_____

_____

_____

5. Who supported your activities as a child? As a young person? As an adult, how do you let others know that you are actively listening?

_____

_____

_____

_____

_____

Leadership Activities—Your Actions

For each of the activities described below, determine what specific steps you will take to complete the activity, a timeline for doing so, and a statement or two about what you hope to accomplish by completing the activity. Finally, indicate what resources you'll need to make it happen.

1. Ask youth to observe people in their world. Can they clearly distinguish between those who are committed to their values and those who aren't? Explore with them how they might connect to adults who are clearly leading value-centered lives.

Action Steps:

Timeline:

Desired Outcomes:

Resources:

2. Invite your group to open their wallets or purses and take out three items. Ask them to turn to the person seated next to them and introduce themselves on the basis of those three items.

   Engage the group in a discussion about their choices using questions like the following. What do your choices say about what's important in your life? Do these items reflect your values or are they just stuff? What else could you include to more accurately demonstrate your values? How do values drive our choices and our actions?

Action Steps:

Timeline:

Desired Outcomes:

_____

Resources:

_____

_____

3. Explore ideas and techniques for asking for support with a group of young people. Demonstrate the networking process and introduce them to people who share their values and interests. Role-play situations where young people practice asking for support.

_____

Action Steps:

_____

Timeline:

_____

Desired Outcomes:

_____

Resources:

_____

4. Work with a young person to prepare and practice a presentation to a group in your community. Attend the event yourself to offer recognition, support, and feedback. Following the event, take time to process how the young person felt about it, what he or she learned by doing it, what could be changed, and what went especially well.

Action Steps:

Timeline:

Desired Outcomes:

Resources:

5. Share with young people a time when your values weren't congruent with your actions. Involve them in a discussion about what they might have done in your place.

Action Steps:

Timeline:

Desired Outcomes:

Resources:

Actions—Your Afterthoughts

After you've carried out each activity or its modification, reflect on the experience using the following guide.

1. What happened when I tried this?

2. What did I learn?

3. What changes will I make the next time I try it?

_____

_____

_____

4. How did these actions help young people to give voice to the leader within?

_____

_____

_____

Chapter Three

Opportunities

Opening Doors to the Community

John Gardner suggests that the opportunities we provide young people should include one or more of the following:[1]

- Opportunities for students to test their judgment under pressure, in the face of opposition, and in the fluid and swiftly changing circumstances so characteristic of action.
- Opportunities to exercise responsibility and perhaps to try out one or another of the skills required for leadership.
- Opportunities for students to test and sharpen their intuitive gifts, and to judge their impact on others.
- Exposure to new "constituencies."
- Exposure to the untidy world, where decisions must be made on inadequate information and the soundest argument doesn't always win, where problems do not get fully solved, or if solved, surface anew in another form.

These types of opportunities are especially the ones that foster leadership because they require more than just doing. They require youth to exercise their brains and their talents for changing

---

[1]John W. Gardner, "Leadership Development," Leadership Papers/7. Independent Sector, June 1987.

their environments and the society around them. They offer excitement through engagement in "real" life.

Through it all, mature, positive, and forward-looking adults act as role models, mentors, coaches, and asset-building champions.

Testing Judgment

A five-year-old asks, "Why?" at everything his grandpa says, and we think it bright or cute. However, if a fifteen-year-old asks, "Why?" after an adult speaks about values or rules, we usually regard it as anything but bright or cute. To the extent that we do not allow the five-year-old and the fifteen-year-old to ask those questions, we stifle the critical thinking process. One of the ways to connect testing judgment and critical thinking is to be constantly willing to explore the "why" question without taking offense or seeing it as a challenge.

Too frequently we talk about the lack of critical judgment and thinking on the part of youth, but the young get there only by practice, just like they get good at skate boarding and singing by practice. To coach a youth along the path to becoming a critical thinker, we need to be ready to answer the "why" question—as well as the "how" question—at every turn. We also need to know what we mean by critical thinking.

In a study of critical thinking, an international group of forty-six experts, using the Delphi Method,[2] arrived at the following consensus statement about critical thinking:

> We understand critical thinking to be purposeful, self-regulatory judgment which results in interpretation, analysis, evaluation, and inference, as well as explanation of the evidential, conceptual, methodological, criteriological, or contextual considerations upon which that judgment is based.

---

[2]Peter A. Facione, *Critical Thinking: What It Is and Why It Counts* (Millbrae, Calif.: Academic Press, 1998).

Now that is a mouthful! Perhaps the group's description of a critical thinker is easier to assimilate:

> That person is habitually inquisitive, well-informed, trustful of reason, open-minded, flexible, fair-minded in evaluation, honest in facing personal biases, prudent in making judgments, willing to reconsider, clear about issues, orderly in complex matters, diligent in seeking relevant information, reasonable in the selection of criteria, focused in inquiry, and persistent in seeking results.

How can we foster those characteristics of critical thinkers in the ways we engage young people? How do we encourage them to be open-minded and honest about their own biases? What opportunities can we provide that give them enough information to make well-informed decisions? How can we encourage them to be reasonable, focused, and persistent?

Critical thinking in youth is not limited to science or politics or economics, but is likely to first be directed to those things the young person knows a lot about: family values, school policies, religious teaching, and the laws of the community. If questions in these areas are not handled in an open, constructive, and "critical" (in a positive sense) spirit, then we are stifling the very quality we seek to instill.

Hannah sees her advanced placement government class as a perfect setting for gaining critical judgment skills. "We discuss many issues that are considered to be 'hot topics,' such as same-sex marriage and abortion," she said. "On this particular topic, I believe that the pro-choice side was much larger than the pro-life side. As the conversation grew, new issues would arise, and students on both sides would increase the intensity of the conversation or give up altogether because they didn't want to face the opposition. This is actually good for both sides because they see how far they are willing to go with their argument." Most important, Hannah said, "It makes a difference in the shaping of your own ideas when you know both sides of the story, and the facts are presented to support them."

Allowing students to explore both sides of an issue in a safe and trusting environment develops character and builds trust. This "practice" in testing judgment pays off when young people need to make immediate, personal decisions on their own.

Two young men were mountain biking in the trails around Lutsen, Minnesota. They came across a platform, and Brent made an instant decision that it was too dangerous to launch himself. On the other hand, his friend took the jump, fell, and tore the ligaments in his leg. When asked how he arrived at his "too dangerous" response, Brent said, "Before taking a risk, I like to visually calculate the risk—see it in my mind's eye. In this case, I didn't see myself making it. The platform was not long enough to make a good approach before launching." Always eager to point out other ways to calculate risk, Brent added, "I suppose I could also have cycled slowly through the path and looked back to determine if the jump was possible."

> *We can also be alert for opportunities for young people to go below the surface—to look for causes and systems involved.*

Exercising Responsibility

Babysitting and doing chores around the house are great ways to teach young people to be responsible early in life. While being paid to babysit and do chores for others makes sense, many parents find that expecting children and youth to do the same things in their own families, without pay, is one way to help them understand the responsibilities that come with being a family member. This expectation can be transferred to any group to which they belong.

Hannah started babysitting for the neighbor kids when she was about twelve. "At that age, it was very important to me that someone would trust me with this huge responsibility," she said. The experience also taught her other leadership skills. "I learned that it is very important to put the needs of others before myself," she reported. "I also learned that you must respect the age/ability/experience of people with whom you are working."

Another family arranged for their daughter, who loved animals, to volunteer at an animal rescue center. There she learned how to care for the animals, and she walked the dogs that were in the center one afternoon a week. Beyond the "doing," she gained an understanding about animals and their care as well as a sense of responsibility.

We can also be alert for opportunities for young people to go below the surface—to look for causes and systems involved. For example, to take it deeper, the parents, or other adults working with the daughter in the animal rescue center, might ask questions similar to the following: Why do dogs need to be rescued? How can we change systems so they don't need to be? What is the process for finding good homes for rescued animals?

Testing and Sharpening Intuitive Gifts and Interest Areas

In order to provide young people with opportunities to use their intuitive gifts, we need first to listen and to watch so that we can recognize their gifts, name them, and affirm them. Being in tune with young people gives them the confidence to act on their intuition.

We can encourage a young person's particular interest area. For example, in planning the youth center for Search Institute's annual Healthy Communities • Healthy Youth Conference, student teams designed and decorated rooms that fit their interests. As a result, the youth center had rooms with a Hollywood theme, a jungle theme, a technology theme, a retro theme, and a game theme.

As a group, the young people, with the encouragement of the youth engagement coordinator, divided into subgroups around their interest. They set the budget (within the context of a larger youth center budget) for their selected rooms, searched local stores for the best buys, shopped, and arranged for transportation of the furnishings.

At the conference, the teams set up the rooms, staffed them, and picked them up each evening. At the end of the event, they packed up and cleaned what was to be saved for future conferences and selected a charity to receive what was left.

In every case, the teams had full responsibility and authority to carry out the project as they deemed appropriate. It was both a skill-building and a leadership experience based on their interests. It resulted in deep pride, a value for teamwork, and a wonderful youth center.

As adults, we can observe the young people within our sphere of interest to help them identify what they are good at and how they might develop skills around their interests. At

Youth themselves understand the need to "get the brothers off the block."

the Search Institute conference, for example, members of the youth involvement team who display a talent for interacting with people, staff the exhibit booth to answer questions and distribute information. Those interested in crafts and artwork design the booth and work in the intergenerational art studio. The goal of the youth coordinator is to provide a variety of activities and experiences to appeal to a broad range of interests. The youth leaders plan every step of the way.

How does the youth adviser know young people's interests? By talking and connecting with them every chance she gets and by truly listening to what they say, their interests are revealed.

Exposure to New Constituencies

Youth themselves understand the need to "get the brothers off the block," as one of the participants in a Minneapolis, Minnesota, neighborhood asset-mapping project put it. They want to be exposed to other ways of doing things and increase their understanding of the world. In our interviews with youth and young adults, travel emerged at the top of the list as an excellent way to find one's identity and explore what to do with one's life. In reflecting back to her travels as a teen, Heather said, "It helps you find out who you are."

Inviting young people to conferences, on field trips, to camps, fairs, and participating with them on service projects are all ways to introduce them to new places, new people, and new ideas. And we can help make those excursions even more meaningful by providing a journal for daily observations. If traveling with a group, you can assign memorable tasks according to the interests of the participants. Some may be the photographers; others the scrapbook compilers; others the mapmakers; others the storytellers or the group musicians.

Then, upon returning from the outing, the young people can be invited to plan a presentation for their peers, a school assembly, younger children, a faith group, or a community organization. Here they generate another skill set: organizing and developing a presentation, giving the presentation, responding to questions, connecting with community leaders, and evaluating the results of the presentation.

Connecting students with different constituencies (communities) can also break down social and economic barriers. Some students from an upper-middle-class area were worried about subsidized housing being built near their school. They weren't sure if they wanted "those" kinds of kids in their neighborhood. Fortunately, one of their teachers learned of their concerns and engaged them in a project to learn about their new neighbors. It brought them in touch with the new families, and as they learned about them, they recognized common interests and activities. As a result, many became fast friends and the worries were eliminated.

Hannah pointed out that her relationship with foreign students in her school helped her to see her own community and the world with "new eyes."

PeaceJam is an international, yearlong, peace education program designed to foster a new generation of peacemakers who take action locally to meet pressing, unmet needs in their schools and neighborhoods through the inspiration of fourteen Nobel Peace Prize laureates. It is intended to promote the development of diverse youth to live healthy and peaceful lives and to possess the attitudes and skills required to meet social, economic, cultural, and political challenges, and to strengthen the fabric of communities by creating local peace projects.

In Minnesota, PeaceJam, hosted by youthrive and the University of St. Thomas, annually brings a very diverse group of young people together for a weekend with a Nobel Peace Prize laureate. They are mixed into "family groups" of ten youth and two college mentors. As a family group, they take part in activities designed to bond their relationships. Family group members reflect together during other parts of the weekend, sharing their thoughts and feelings on issues important to them. This family group experience helps young people see things through different lenses and opens their own eyes to new possibilities for creating communities of peace.

Exposure to the Untidy World

The world is indeed untidy. We are a society hungry for inspiring leaders, people who are willing to stand up and use their influence for the greater good. We need the leadership, brainpower, energy, imagination, and talent that young people can offer. Exposure to the untidy world strengthens their resolve and sharpens the skill sets needed for situations when their entire energy and commitment to a cause go sour.

> *We are a society hungry for inspiring leaders, people who are willing to stand up and use their influence for the greater good.*

A young leader at a youth conference was deeply committed to the 2004 Kerry presidential campaign and spent hours working to get out the vote. When she learned that John Kerry wasn't elected, she was devastated, really wounded. Her adviser realized that the young leader needed to be with people who could offer the greatest comfort, her family. While driving the young woman home, the adviser became aware that when young people give so much of themselves and it doesn't work out, adults need to be around to recognize their loss, be prepared for their emotional response, and help them understand that just because—in this case—Kerry lost, it didn't mean that they had to give up on the issues that attracted them in the first place. It didn't mean that the energy expended was wasted. A cause was advanced; awareness of the issues was expanded; more people voted—all important results.

All leaders face disappointment; the mark of a true leader is to learn from it and become stronger in the process.

When we encourage young people to speak out, give of themselves, and pour their passion into a project, we also need to stand by their side when the world demonstrates its untidy self. We can build in ways to make a disappointment easier to bear when we say, "Let's talk about what happens if . . ." Or by asking, "If this happens, what will you do?" Envisioning the future often softens the impact of disappointment.

When young people experience disappointment for the first time, they feel it more deeply, take it more personally, perhaps than adults. They simply haven't the life experience to realize that they will recover from disappointment over time.

Another way to help young people deal with disappointment is to explore what worked and what didn't, and what could be done differently a second time around. All leaders face disappointment; the mark of a true leader is to learn from it and become stronger in the process.

Adults have to be involved in young people's lives in a way that makes youth feel safe and secure and trusted. For example, one issue is the "Code of Silence" that seems to prevail when students know that something or someone is potentially dangerous and do not report it. In cases of school shooting sprees that have gained national attention, studies indicate that a number of students knew about the potential for violence before it happened. In a report cited in the *Minneapolis StarTribune,* these "bystanders" offered Secret Service interviewers various reasons for not coming forward: they didn't want to be seen as "snitches"; they had doubts that the shooter was serious; and they were uncertain how their information would be used.[3]

Too often, young people think their peer is simply "blowing off steam," or as one of the young people said, "just talking shit." We can help young people understand that when their peers are talking in this way, they can offer to explore the reasons for the negative expression and suggest support in the form of counseling or connection with a caring adult. They should also talk to a caring adult themselves.

In this untidy world, we need to let young people know that they are accountable for the actions and decisions they make, and that we will use whatever information comes to us in a responsible way. We need to let them know that we are morally obligated to report what, in our judgment, is critical to the safety and well-being of others. (It helps to be specific about what we will report and to whom.) At the same time, we need to assure young people that they have made the right decision when they share information with us.

Where Do You Find These Opportunities?

Opportunities for leadership occur throughout the community. As you think about them, pay attention to religious holidays and practices and avoid scheduling events or activities that may interfere. In cases where you are not in control of the dates or venues, accommodate the practices of young people who might be involved. For example, you may need to offer particular foods, set specific times to eat, or designate a special place apart in which to pray. Check with the young people in your group about their needs before you begin. Remember, it's all about respect. Know, really know, the youth with whom you are working and what is important to them.

---

[3]Chuck Haga, "Why Wouldn't Someone Speak Up? Lots of Reasons," *Minneapolis Star Tribune,* February 1, 2006.

Community Volunteer/Faith-based Service

Volunteering often helps young people discover who they are as people and what they want to be as well as what they want to give to others. It contributes to self-efficacy, boosting motivation, optimism, and self-regulation. It's a way to connect their spirit to a way of living. "Volunteering takes the center of their world and expands their world," said Heather. "They get a true sense of their value by watching change happen in their communities."

Volunteering takes many forms during a person's lifetime, and the experiences we have as children and young people shape us for lifetimes of service, both formal and informal. Adults can provide opportunities, support, and space for young people to develop what the French social philosopher Alexis de Tocqueville called "habits of the heart" when he described American moral attitudes and customs in the 1830s.

Many school- and faith-based organizations offer service or "mission" trips or projects to help those in need. (However, undertaking such a trip to "find out how good he or she has it" is the wrong reason for young people to get involved.) When young people are engaged in planning the experience, they learn valuable leadership and organizational skills. When they are given the opportunity to identify an issue and explore ways to provide support, they learn even more. As a result, they gain a great feeling of accomplishment and see themselves as valued community leaders.

Volunteering gives young people purpose. It is a way to connect them with people outside their sphere of interest/influence, and it can change their perspective! For example, young people who were having problems in school were assigned a service-learning project in an Alzheimer's unit in a long-term care facility. They knew nothing about the disease and had never had contact with people who no longer had a sense of reality. Their task was to work with the residents three hours per week and follow up with research on the disease in order to inform and educate others and to help family members better understand the disease and their loved one's current situation. Upon completion of the project, all of the students remained with the program as family educators, as care volunteers, and as spokespeople for groups who wanted to learn more about Alzheimer's disease. Not surprisingly, their new knowledge and change of heart led to a decrease in problems at school.

Family Volunteering

The continuum of service often begins with what many people call "acts of kindness." They usually start when parents involve their children in their own acts of kindness in a community—bringing donations to the local food shelf, shopping for a toy for another child at Christmastime, visiting a sick or frail elder. Sometimes these acts of kindness can turn into real life changers, or lifesavers, as you read in the case of Haley and Jack. In fact, the National Survey of Volunteering and Giving Among Teenagers, launched by Independent Sector and conducted by the Gallup Organization in 1996, reports that volunteering is more likely to become a lifetime habit when children are exposed to concepts of caring, sharing, and community at an early age.

Schools

Many of the young people we interviewed said they started volunteering as young children alongside their parents. For others, school provided the first opportunity to lead. Participation in student government was a primary activity. It gave them confidence in their leadership abilities and provided opportunities to serve as a voice for young people in other ways.

As a first-year high school student, Erko learned that his school had been unfairly put on academic probation a few years prior to his attendance. Seeing some of the students in the upper grades organizing to get rid of the label "sparked his fire," and he joined the protest. They went to school board hearings, wrote letters, and got the word out. As a result of their student efforts, the label was finally lifted.

Outside of student government, some schools offer opportunities for tutoring, peer counseling/mediation, and coaching—both in sports and in the arts. In their interaction with their peers, or with younger children, young people can assess their own skills and transmit them to others.

While we will talk about the benefits of knitting and other crafts in chapter 4, one of the latest rages among both girls and boys is teaching others to knit and crochet. The young people first learn this new skill from their moms, grandparents, community education classes, or at yarn/craft shops. Once "hooked," they gather interested youth in their schools and communities into clubs to learn to knit.

Across the nation, a number of youth-run small businesses have evolved from this phenomenon. Other knitting clubs, led by teens, are creating scarves, hats, and other cold-weather garments for shelters, hospitals, church programs, and sports teams!

Here are two more examples of school opportunities. Charlene was born a cocaine addict, and at age three she was removed from her mother's care. She was dyslexic (a learning condition caused by the drugs she had been exposed to). She exhibited violent tendencies in elementary school and was expelled. Her penchant for being a bully made her popular with other kids who terrorized their peers. Charlene was given an opportunity to be in peer mediation rather than permanently expelled from school. She went through the program and became one of the school's best mediators. Charlene affirms that the peer mediation program changed her life—it kept her in school, she bonded with teachers and other staff, and today she is completing her college education.

For their PeaceJam service-learning project, a group of young people at the Afrocentric Educational Academy, a Minneapolis, Minnesota, middle school, conducted a survey with their adviser, Anne Parish. Their task was to identify whether and what types of violence were occurring in the school. Through survey responses, they determined that preventing specific forms of violence such as bullying, gossiping, and teasing was a significant concern of their peers. To counteract these negative behaviors, the young leaders held four all-school assemblies to talk about the issues and ways to prevent violence in the future. To measure the impact of their peace project, the young people planned a post-survey to determine how the school environment changed.

School activities are valuable to young people, especially when they back up their confidence and experience with knowledge, as was seen in the story of young people working in the Alzheimer's unit. Many schools offer service-learning classes in which students identify projects they want to do to improve the communities in which they live.

Leadership goes hand in hand with service-learning. Again, according to the Independent Sector/Gallup poll, students who took a service-learning class said that they learned how to solve community problems, understand more about good citizenship, became aware of community programs, and learned more about how government and voluntary organizations worked. They also learned to better understand people that were different from themselves.

Effective service-learning provides students with an opportunity to participate in thoughtfully organized experiences. Generally speaking, strong, effective service-learning projects will:

- Meet actual community needs;
- Coordinate school and community members who will benefit from the services;
- Be integrated into academic curriculum;
- Provide structured time for students to think, talk. present, or write about what they saw and did to deepen understanding of the cause or need being met;
- Measure whether students met their learning goals; and
- Foster a sense of caring for others.

For further information, check out the national service-learning clearinghouse Web site (www.servicelearning.org).

Community Organizations at the Local, State, and National Levels

Volunteering with community organizations also provides leadership opportunities for young people. According to the poll mentioned earlier, teens volunteer 2.4 billion hours annually. They choose to volunteer because they feel compassion for people in need, they can do something for a cause in which they believe, and they believe that if they can help others, others will help them. They go on to learn to respect others, how to get along with and relate to others, and to understand people who are different from themselves. They become better people as a result of their volunteering, learn new skills, and become more tolerant of others.

Involvement in community organizations is also a great way to help immigrant youth understand American culture while sharing their own cultural experiences with others.

Adults can build on young people's compassion and passion to influence and improve their communities if they recognize youth as resources to be empowered, not problems to be solved. We can begin by asking their opinions, recognizing their input, and following their lead. The most critical first step is simply to ask them to volunteer— all of them.

Young people gain leadership skills when they are involved in environmental activities such as cleaning up or improving parks and recreational facilities, or when they participate in cultural activities such as theater productions, music, and arts groups. As leaders, they can also serve on nonprofit boards of directors and engage in youth philanthropy. Through these higher-level experiences, young people can contribute their personal resources, plan, implement, and even fund-raise for materials and supplies for their projects as well as their organizations.

Young people are naturally attracted to projects that take into consideration their time and their interests and that are known for building strong relationships. At the same time that we support the leadership development of young people at the local level, we can also look for ways to involve them in leadership roles at the state and national levels.

Maya began volunteering in middle school. She was appointed co-chair, along with the lieutenant governor and Mike, of the Minnesota Alliance with Youth in her junior year of high school, and volunteered at a juvenile correctional facility after high school. As a college student and Truman Scholar, Maya founded a public service journal, *The Bridge,* and organized the University Promise Alliance at the University of Minnesota to mobilize students and communities in various service projects. During this time, she also served initially on the America's Promise youth partnership team (see www.americaspromise.org).

In recognition of her leadership voice, Maya was then invited to become a full-fledged board member for America's Promise. In October of 2004, she was named one of the Top Ten College Women by *Glamour* magazine. Today Maya is enrolled in Harvard Medical School and is pursuing a master's degree in business administration at the same university.

In addition to acquiring leadership skills through direct service, young people also learn from being involved in organizational governance. This form of participation demands special attention. When we invite young people to serve on committees or boards of directors, we need to make certain that their roles are not segmented or token but are integral to the workings of the organization as a whole. Youth board members need to know that they matter as much as the adult in the next chair. Inviting two or more youth to serve on a board at one time is critical. It gives them confidence and a greater sense that they aren't a lone voice, but a collective voice.

As a youth member of youthrive's board of directors, Frannie approved the mission and vision and set the goals for the fledgling organization. She served on the youth leadership team that helped select both the organization's name and its logo and chairs the communications committee. As a board member, Frannie has an equal vote with adult members in guiding the nonprofit organization. She is particularly watchful that every level of youthrive engages youth as leaders and that all of its programming values and reflects youth voice. After all, the organization's mission is to engage young people with adults in strengthening leadership and peace-building skills.

"Serving on the board of directors of youthrive has given me the wonderful experience of working with both youth and adults of all ages," Frannie said. "It has also opened my eyes to all the other ways youth can contribute to the community. We are all learning and growing from one another. We are also making wonderful relationships that will overall help our organization grow."

If we are asking young people to give time and energy, we need to be respectful of their other commitments. We need to know their individual situations before asking them to serve. If they are taking time off from work, for example, can we somehow compensate them for lost wages, or meet with their employers ahead of time to see if they can have paid time off for leadership volunteer activities? Many corporations allow release time for their adult employees to do service in the community. Why not young

> *If we are asking young people to give time and energy, we need to be respectful of their other commitments.*

people as well? Together with the young person, arm yourself with examples of the benefits the experience will "return" to the workplace (see chapter 5). Then approach the manager—with the student's permission, of course. An alternative is to coach the young person to make the "ask" without you. You simply remain available to respond to questions.

If students are taking time away from school, an adviser can write a letter to the school principal explaining how the students' leadership roles will contribute to their learning and understanding of the world around them. The adviser can also point out the possibility of the students receiving community awards for their service and the value of community service on college, job, and scholarship applications and career résumés.

Volunteering provides a testing ground for leadership because so many opportunities are available. And, according to Will, adult volunteers have time to help develop a young person's skills in a way that people on time clocks do not.

Government

Many state and local governments are required by law to include youth on their advisory councils or boards. Others simply invite them to become part of their deliberations, especially on issues related to youth. Opportunities vary according to location.

Kirkland, Washington, includes a young person, between the ages of sixteen and eighteen as a voting member on city boards and commissions that deal the most with youth issues. Among Minnesota's 340 school districts, at least 60 report having students on their boards. According to a *Minneapolis Star Tribune* story, the students may not have a vote on budgets, hiring decisions, and other management issues, but they do provide insights that adult members say they value.[4]

In fact, another article in the *Minneapolis Star Tribune* cited several Minnesota cities as being great places for youth.[5] Key to their nomination for this status was the availability of leadership opportunities for young people in government agencies. Mankato has young people serving on city and school committees, and Olmsted County and Rochester have a youth commission on which an equal number of youth and adults work together to solve community problems.

If similar opportunities aren't available in your community, think about how you might partner with local agencies and with youth to establish advisories to various government bodies.

---

[4]Dan Wascoe, "In Some Districts, Students Pick Their Representatives," *Minneapolis Star Tribune*, February 5, 2005.
[5]"Where Is IT At? St. Louis Park," *Minneapolis Star Tribune*, September 27, 2005.

Volunteering and leadership experience open other types of opportunities for young people. Many young people, active in their communities, are selected for awards and forms of recognition for their service. Others need to understand how to access and use these experiences for building résumés for both college and job applications. They often point young people in the direction of careers that match their interests and passions. As a result of his leadership experiences, for example, Via served as a board member of Hmong College Students of Minnesota (HCSM), providing academic, social, and networking support for his peers and younger students. "I chose to be on this board," Via told us, "because I like the opportunity HCSM provides. I also wanted to help younger Hmong generations achieve a better education because that was what I once wished for. Now that I am more mature and educated, I want to reach out to as many Hmong students as possible to guide them on their journey to becoming someone great for themselves."

By volunteering and being engaged in leadership opportunities, young people are able to experiment with potential career choices and explore options for ways to live their lives to the fullest. For example, one of the students in Marlys's January-term class on nonprofit management at Gustavus Adolphus College shared her desire to go to medical school but said that after serving on a national youth board for her church, she also felt called to work for a nonprofit organization.

Reflections—Your Thoughts and Inspirations

Taking time to reflect on our experiences deepens our learning. It fosters critical thinking and analysis. Use the following suggestions to gain new insight into your own experiences, articulate them in writing, and apply that awareness to connect more effectively with young people.

1. What types of opportunities did you have as a young person that involved you in meaningful roles? How did adults encourage you to step forward?

How did they discourage you, either overtly or subtly? In what manner did they make the opportunities available to you?

_____

_____

_____

_____

_____

2. What types of activities do you wish had been available to you as a young person? How would those activities have made a difference for you as an adult? How can you translate your experiences to the current generation?

_____

_____

_____

_____

_____

3. Do you think John Gardner was on point when he described opportunities for young people? Why or why not? Which of his statements especially resonated for you?

_____

_____

_____

_____

_____

4. Consider a recent experience when you had to make a choice. How did you decide? What did you do? Did you make the right choice? How can you

share this example with young people? How can we bring our own values into a situation without being judgmental?

_____

_____

_____

_____

_____

5. Young people appreciate and value being asked for their ideas and opinions. Think about the community or faith-based organizations to which you are connected. What issue or topic will benefit from a youth voice? How will you turn this into an authentic leadership experience?

_____

_____

_____

_____

_____

6. What boundaries did you have as a young person that guided your behavior? Are those same boundaries in place for today's generation? How are they the same or different? Will the young people with whom you work benefit from this type of discussion?

_____

_____

_____

_____

_____

Leadership Activities—Your Actions

For each of the activities described below, determine what specific steps you will take to complete the activity, a timeline for doing so, and a statement or two about what you hope to accomplish by completing the activity. Finally, indicate what resources you'll need to make it happen.

1. Using your leadership and listening skills, draw out from a group of young people the needs in the community that really trigger their interest. Help them to create a new response or opportunity—one not currently available in your community—based on their own interests and passions.

Action Steps:

Timeline:

Desired Outcomes:

Resources:

2. Schedule a time to meet with your city council. Ahead of this time, work with youth to discover and become knowledgeable on issues facing the community. Have them select one in which they are interested and support their efforts to map out a plan of action and take it directly to the council.

Action Steps:

Timeline:

Desired Outcomes:

Resources:

3. Make certain to connect with persons from all cultural groups in your community. Independent Sector found that people are four times more likely to volunteer if they are asked, yet minority groups are not asked at the same rate majority groups are. How will you make this connection happen? Where might you have current relationships on which to build and expand? How will you involve young people in the process?

Action Steps:

Timeline:

Desired Outcomes:

Resources:

4. Visit with your local faith communities, schools, and organizations to determine what opportunities are available to young people. Then connect the young people in your sphere of influence with those opportunities that fit their particular gifts and interests.

Action Steps:

Timeline:

Desired Outcomes:

Resources:

5. Work with young people to identify and reach out to a group in the school or community that may be isolated. Working together, plan an activity or project to promote understanding and build relationships. Host the activity at a school or community center. Reflect on how it felt to build understanding and how it changed attitudes in the school or community. Talk about how to continue or sustain the project.

Action Steps:

Timeline:

Desired Outcomes:

Resources:

6. Once young people have identified opportunities that are readily accessible, help make it possible by providing transportation, making connections, and offering other types of support as needed.

Action Steps:

Timeline:

Desired Outcomes:

Resources:

Actions—Your Afterthoughts

After you've carried out each activity or its modification, reflect on the experience using the following guide.

1. What happened when I tried this?

2. What did I learn?

3. What changes will I make the next time I try it?

_____

_____

_____

4. How did these actions help young people to give voice to the leader within?

_____

_____

_____

Chapter Four

Space

Establishing a Place *to Be*

Space to give voice to the leader comes within two parameters. The first is external space that allows young people to do things on their own with the opportunity to make decisions and learn from them. External space is the environment for trial and error—a safe space, warm and nurturing—a place where it is okay to be who they are with no pretense or pressure. In this space, young people feel comfortable taking positive risks—reaching out and sharing who they are and what they dream. It's an environment in which they can grow, learn, and try new things. External space can also be physical—a space that young people help to create and where they feel ownership.

The second is internal space where young people take time for personal reflection and study—a space where they take time to feed the spirit, the soul, and the voice of the leader within. Often, it takes reflection—connecting the internal to the external—to arrive at meaningful results. This is the place where young people find their internal compasses and examine their place in the world around them.

External Space

Make Mistakes and Learn from Them

As much as we want to protect young people from making mistakes and as hard as it is not to tell them what to do, we need to be careful about interfering too much in their lives as they seek to soar as independent beings.

Mike echoes Michael's story (see chapter 2). "Sometimes," he reported, "young people need to make mistakes in order to learn and develop their own style of leading." While Michael was in jail, he had the space to think about and reflect on his actions and when his mom said, "From now on your life is in your hands," he was given the space to continue making mistakes or to take his experience and turn it around.

External space is the environment for trial and error.

Erko suggests that adults should not hand everything to young people. "They can help," he said, "but they need to ease off sometimes, allowing us to find things out and learn on our own." Callie described this tendency of adults to overprotect as "smothering."

"To know that an adult has confidence in your idea makes you more confident and gives you space to become a leader," said Will.

Being Open and Flexible

The Millennials are characterized as being collaborative, open to diversity, and wanting flexibility in their volunteer activities. However, they also appreciate clearly defined tasks and assignments. How do these characteristics play out in giving voice to the leader within?

"As a leader, you can't possible know everything," said Mike. "Therefore, you need to cooperate with others to find the right decision." Teams and teamwork are critical modes of operation for this age group, and this often demands openness and flexibility so that the team can move forward.

Young people find that being open and flexible brings rewards. For example, Callie is all for working in groups with other youth. She feels it allows them to bounce ideas off one another. "As a leader, I am excited to hear what others have to contribute," she reported. "I look forward to what will happen when my ideas are combined with others. Leaders must realize that so much can be accomplished—not individually—but when people work together. What might seem like a wonderful idea can be made even better when enhanced by another person's outlook!"

Mike suggested that "any leader must be willing to listen to all viewpoints and ideas, be able to get people engaged and energized, and be able to manage their time well."

Maya found that being open-minded and willing to cross boundaries of all sorts are two of the skills, talents, or attributes critical to

> *"To know that an adult has confidence in your idea makes you more confident and gives you space to become a leader."*

leadership. To this list, she added persistence and pragmatism combined with the ability to recognize leadership qualities in others and delegate responsibility. She admitted, however, that she struggled with delegating "because there are so many with whom I work who don't know their qualities and strengths."

According to Maya, adults can help young people gain skills in these and other areas by giving positive feedback, being respectful of their schedules, and showing interest in and appreciation of their lives and talents.

Evolving Your Own Ideas without Judgment

Creativity in young people is enhanced when adults respect their ideas and give them the latitude to follow through with their concepts from beginning to end. Being able to act out his ideas in his own surroundings is important to Via. "I like being able to express myself in a way that I created it—like being funny or just serious," he said. It's important to Via that no one judge him in advance and tell him that his ideas won't work.

"I give voice to the leader within me," said Callie, "by approaching new and exciting opportunities with an open mind."

Trust and Respect

Creating a bridge of trust and respect with young people is one of life's great gifts. It also engenders a huge responsibility toward the young people who rely on us. We need to be ever vigilant not to betray that confidence and to constantly reinforce, by our behaviors, respect for the young people with whom we come in contact.

> *Creating a bridge of trust and respect with young people is one of life's great gifts.*

In building this bridge, youth leaders stress the importance of discovering what turns young people on and identifying what they want to explore. "Make it easy for them to connect with you," said Nicky Metchnek, a school social worker. "Let them know they are appreciated and loved."

In describing the various generational differences in shaping leadership, Merrill Associates wrote: "In an era of complicity and change, young people look for leaders who work with followers as intimate allies. They want colleagues who will develop relationships that build intimacy and show trust and respect for them, their abilities, and their ideas."[1]

We forge trust and respect when we allow young people to give voice to their passions without interjecting our ideas on the topic. Rather, we need to ask the questions that allow young people to express their thoughts and feelings openly.

According to Rabbi Simeon Glaser of Minneapolis, Minnesota, empowering young people to express their own ideas is critical. "Validation is more important than intellectual growth," he said. He also added these words of wisdom: "Never shame or embarrass young people in front of their peers. They will be done with you forever!"

Rabbi Glaser works hard to relate to young people in ways

[1]Merrill Associates, "Five Generational Differences Shaping Leadership," Topic of the Month, August 2004 (www.merrillassociates.com).

that will engender their respect and affection, in part because he was not very connected as a teen. "I want them to like me," he said. "And when one wants to be liked, you work hard to understand kids, to discover what turns them on and what they want to explore."

He went on to say, "There is a Hebrew word, *ḥidush*, which means 'new idea.' Teens have so many ḥidushes that adults need to hear, to pay attention to, and pursue with the kids."

> *"Never shame or embarrass young people in front of their peers."*

Trust and respect are not just acts between adults and youth. As these important concepts are internalized, they create personal power. Samantha told us that internal power comes when she feels respected and complimented by others. According to her, leaders need to have self-respect and believe in themselves before they can connect with a group. "Without it, you simply cannot get your idea across," she asserted.

Young people are usually open and comfortable in conversations and easily "warm up" to a relationship when adults are also open. They see our openness when we make eye contact, smile, say "hello." These greetings are enhanced when accompanied by a personal comment that demonstrates that we are truly interested. Or when we ask a question that requires interaction. Adults need to start at a place of trust and respect and proceed from there. If you are aloof, it will set up barriers and hinder communications, and you will have to work all that much harder.

Physical Space

Youth love a place to be with their peers—somewhere "to hang." Whether it is a room in a place of worship, a youth-serving or other community agency or community facility, having a place to call their own is important. Here they can establish guidelines, decorate as they choose, and plan the programming. It's a place they can just *be*.

One of the unique examples we found was the Peace Palace Project in a diverse Minneapolis neighborhood. In addition to being a place "to hang," the Peace Palace was a place that gathered people across generations.

The Peace Palace came into existence when an unused commercial space was made available to Redeemer Lutheran Church. The church developed the space, and it served as a dedicated neighborhood resource to promote peace and nonviolence. The facility was a supervised place for adults, children, youth, and families to meet and experience a healthy community. People of all ages, who had not been traditionally connected, found the Peace Palace a place to play together, volunteer together, and take pride in a sense of ownership.

Our experience suggests that when youth are actively engaged in the planning, implementation, and delivery of services, they become stakeholders in the process and part of the solution rather than part of the problem.

The Depot Coffee House in Hopkins, Minnesota, was the outgrowth of a forum sponsored by the city's Chemical Health Commission. At that forum, held in 1996 and attended by approximately 250 community members, thirteen young people presented their stories. Some of the youth had never used, many were in recovery, some were narcotic dependent or suffered from chronic alcoholism or smoking addiction. The community was amazed by the young people's stories, and it became obvious that Hopkins did not have a safe and chemically free place for youth to gather.

Community members, businesspeople, and students worked together to resolve the dilemma. An abandoned train depot in a great location, with historical restoration potential and a one-dollar yearly lease to the city of Hopkins from the Regional Railroad Authority, was selected as the site. The renovation was completed by volunteers and funded by contributions of money, labor, materials, and grants from area foundations. The doors opened on September 2, 1998.

The mission of the Depot, as it is called, is "to enhance community unity and create a student experience in a chemically-free environment fostering communication and building a bridge of respect between students and the greater community." Except for Friday evenings, when the focus is high school students, the Depot is open to the general public for coffee breaks, business meetings, and private rental for parties.

Governance of the Depot is by "student decisions with adult guidance," and a student board of directors meets weekly. The board of directors currently comprises thirteen students and three adults.

Student artwork is encouraged and displayed. Local music groups are welcome to play at the Depot. Additionally, the building houses a learning lab for the school district's business department.

Internal Space

Journaling

Introducing journaling to young people can be a profound way for them to find inner space. Journaling is a safe and private way for each of us, regardless of age, to express what is in our hearts and minds. Oftentimes it is therapeutic, and it offers us a unique perspective on our own lives, especially when we take time to reflect on what we have written, perhaps not immediately, but days or months or even years later.

> *Internal space [is] where young people take time for personal reflection and study—a space where they take time to feed the spirit, the soul, and the voice of the leader within.*

Journaling is a useful route to self-knowledge that benefits people of all ages. When engaged in a journaling activity with young people, adults can establish common ground by journaling at the same time. When Marlys takes her grandchildren on special trips, they journal together at the end of the day. This activity often leads to a deeper discussion of their experiences and to the recognition that each of them sees the day from a different perspective. When the larger family gets together, the journals are often a great source for storytelling.

Young men at the Minnesota Correctional Facility–Red Wing (MCF-Red Wing) are introduced to journaling shortly after their incarceration begins. It is an important part of the healing process for the fourteen- to nineteen-year-old youth. As you read the following stories, you can see how journaling helped them get their feelings out. They were able to expand on their ideas and experiences and put them in perspective, and they learned the value of journaling enough to continue it. Their journaling gave them a wonderful way to remember, reflect, and gain satisfaction.

- **Getting It Out**

"Putting my thoughts on paper got them out of my head. There were times when I had many thoughts running through my head and they just went on and on and around and around. During the day I could deal with this, but at night it prevented me from getting to sleep. Even though I was tired, writing in my journal helped to get these thoughts out of my head. Then I would find my mind calmer to the point of being able to fall asleep."

"Writing when sad gets the sadness out."

"Writing in my journal about my anger with someone, particularly a friend, helped to get the anger out and away from me, onto the paper. Seeing it on paper seemed to place it somewhere else other than in me. Though it did not completely go away, it was lessened quite a bit. Sometimes putting it on paper helped me to see why the action upset me so much. Sometimes I could see that the action was not intentional when seeing it written down, and that helped a lot. Writing, no matter how fast it is done, is slower than the time taken to be offended or to react to an action or word by a friend or acquaintance, and in that slowed-down time, I see things differently."

"If I write an angry letter or note to someone, I am able to say all those things that I would never think of saying if face to face. And what I write can be made so much more hurtful because I can use really good words, and I know that when they read it, they can go over it again and again like I am saying it over and over again. But by the time I read it over after finishing it (I always read over it because I want to hear how it sounds after it is all together), I think twice about sending it because it sounds so mean. I usually feel better after writing it, but then am faced with sending it. I've spent a lot of time and energy, especially if I'm really mad, and it doesn't make sense not to send it, but I've always got the choice and, no matter if I send it or not, I've gotten the anger out of my system. That's the best part of writing the angry letter. And sometimes I've written some pretty good stuff when angry."

"Being lonely is not so severe when I've written about it. It seems like someone has listened to me."

"I can write anything I want. I don't have to be concerned about what I say or how I say it. The grammar is unimportant. Sometimes it's just a stream of words. Probably makes sense only to me."

- **Expanding on It**

"With my journaling, I am able to expand on ideas which otherwise would be like a stray thought. It's like writing forces the brain to focus on an idea. Even a single sentence can turn into two by the time the first one is finished."

"When something important has happened, I write about it. It can be good or bad important, but writing about it makes it even more important because I dwell on it in a different way than just talking about it. And it seems that when I see it in writing, especially in my own words, it takes on even more importance. I do not write about too much bad stuff because that takes on even more meaning and seems to stick with me in a bigger way than the way the good stuff sticks with me."

- **Putting It in Perspective**

"Whenever I write about almost anything, I tend to write about both sides of an issue, even if I just want to write about my reasons for doing something. When writing I dwell on things a little longer than when just talking about them, or thinking about them, and the reasons for not doing something have time to enter my mind, and I just write about them as well. So I end up with a bunch of reasons all mixed together and in the end have a perspective I had not intended. Usually this is good, but sometimes I am angry at myself for changing my mind because I put my thoughts in writing."

"I've been able to sort out my feelings by writing about them."

"Sometimes I actually make a list of pros and cons when considering a course of action. This is really a structured thing like school and not as easy as just writing about what is going through my head, but it has helped a lot when I've got a really big decision to make."

"Journaling helps me look at myself and not make some of the same mistakes."

- **Continuing It**

"When I've had a really good day or experience or time, I love to write about it in my journal. I like to talk to my friends about it too, but it is not the same as writing because I am able to focus on it. It's like continuing the experience, the good feelings, the excitement and the joy. Doing the writing and seeing the words just seem to force the experience to continue and this makes me want to write even more. With friends I run the risk of getting some negative feedback, but with writing I never get anything negative."

- **Remembering It**

"Sometimes I have a lot of things to remember, things to do, and I just can't seem to keep them all in my head. So, I write them down. Then I have only one thing to remember. And when I look at the list, it always seems like it will be easier to get everything done than when all that stuff was just floating around in my head."

"Journaling is comforting—a big release."

"At the end of the day, I like to jot down the things I've done that day. I like the feeling of satisfaction I get by looking at all I've done. Some days there is really big stuff like graduation, but the list can always be filled with stuff I've done with food or outside. Sometimes I look at my list of regular stuff, like brushing my teeth on a slow day, and realize that life is composed of a lot of regular stuff."

Mindfulness

Being mindful is bringing one's full attention to the present without judgment, without reflection, without thought. You are simply observing the moment in which you find yourself. You are there with no other purpose than being aware of that particular point in time. In the introduction to his book *Wherever You Go, There You Are,* MIT-trained molecular biologist Jon Kabat-Zinn says, "Wherever you go, there you are. Whatever you wind up doing, *that's* what's on your mind . . . we all too easily conduct our lives as if forgetting momentarily that we are *here*, where we already are, and that we are in what we are already *in*."[2]

Mindfulness breeds curiosity and creativity in response to the question, "What's going on right here, right now?" It offers a sense of acceptance and tolerance. It's an opportunity to step back from the messiness of daily life to center oneself and gain a new perspective.

For example, the yoga teacher asks her participants to focus on their breath and invites them to "be now here, in this moment." They are not in the past nor in the future—to be so would have them miss out on what may be the only moment they have. She reminds them that to move the "w" from the end of "now" to the beginning of the word "here," suggests that if they are not "now here," they are "no where."

U.S. Poet Laureate Ted Kooser, of Garland, Nebraska, has said, "We're too bombarded by the past and the future. Very seldom are we right in the moment. That's where we have to be."

Yoga instructors and others who teach meditation and mindfulness stress the importance of focusing first on the breath. Focusing starts by breathing gently through the nose and letting the abdomen drop and expand, followed by breathing out and tightening the abdomen against the back wall of the body. Think of how ocean waves roll onto a beach. As soon as one fades out, another rushes in. The movement is continuous. It comes and goes, its rhythm akin to the phrase, "The tide rises, the tide falls," from the Henry Wadsworth Longfellow poem by the same title.

By helping young people understand and practice mindfulness, we provide them with a tool that puts them a little more in control of their lives and an effective way to handle stress. As one youth described yoga, "You don't think about much crap

---

[2]Jon Kabat-Zinn, *Wherever You Go, There You Are: Mindfulness Meditation in Everyday Life* (New York: Hyperion, 1994), page xiii.

when you are holding poses or in difficult positions. Yoga is tough but really good for your mind."

One of the ways we can help young people incorporate this meaningful practice is to become mindful ourselves. A broad array of books and descriptive materials are available through public libraries, doctors' offices, and health clinics. Meditation can be done informally on your own or through classes led by instructors experienced in a variety of techniques. Two books that may be of interest are *Blue Jean Buddha: Voices of Youth Buddhists,* edited by Sumi Loundon (Wisdom Publications, 2001), and *Teaching Meditation to Children: A Practical Guide to the Use and Benefits of Meditation Techniques,* by David Fontana and Ingrid Slack (Element Books, 1998).

If you are uncomfortable sharing this knowledge with the young people in your environment, invite a yoga instructor or other mindfulness practitioners to meet with your group and share the basics of focusing on the moment, of focusing on breath. In fact, a growing number of schools, as well as clinics, are offering formal programs on mind, body, and spirit.

If he had his way, David Lynch, writer and director of *The Elephant Man, Blue Velvet, Twin Peaks,* and other funky productions, transcendental meditation lessons would be placed in every American classroom for any students who wanted them. "In the classroom where meditation has been taught," Lynch says, "you'll see students much happier, much brighter, eager to learn."[3]

Introducing yoga to young people is a "hands on" way to help them move inward. Once they begin a yoga practice, they are able to make better decisions because they know what's going on in their minds and their bodies. Paying attention to their breath and the sensations in their bodies reduces their anxieties, anger, and uncertainties. It also teaches them to focus—a handy skill when it comes to test preparation!

---

[3]Bill Newcott, "Inside Man: David Lynch Teaches Meditation," *AARP,* July–August, 2006.

Whatever the method, we must remember that when we introduce young people to mindfulness practice, we are giving them time and space to pay attention to their own thoughts and movements.

The results can be spectacular. While mindfulness promotes self-growth and wellness, it also affects the people around us. It allows us to let go of our expectations for people, knowing that just loving them for what they are promotes their own sense of self and inner peace.

When parents and adults are mindful of the present—really paying attention to the young person in front of them—they are able to let go of their own expectations, judgments, and ideas. In focusing on acceptance of self and others, they become more compassionate. They give young people the space to be who they are.

Another form of mindfulness is T'ai Chi Chih® or Joy through Movement. T'ai Chi Chih is the Westernized version of the Chinese T'ai Chi, a series of twenty movement patterns that generate, circulate, and harmonize internal energy flow. Its purpose is to circulate the Chi, our Vital Force energy, and the movements are meant to be practiced in the most relaxed state possible.

Jackie practices T'ai Chi Chih and feels that it covers both external and internal space. The external space is the one used to practice the movements, outside by water when possible, and the internal space is the relaxed and meditative mind. The movements are soft, slow, and even without effort. "One of the greatest outcomes of this practice," says Jackie, "is the balance of body, mind, and spirit." If you are interested in learning more, check out the Web sites www.worldtaichiday.org or www.taichichih.org.

Prayer

Regardless of personal religious affiliation, prayer can play a powerful role in the lives of young people, especially when they are given the freedom and encouragement to express themselves through prayer.

Prayer can be thought of as personal talks with someone or

something that is greater than oneself, a listener who doesn't interrupt the flow of conversation. Prayer is a way to bring joys, sorrows, challenges, burdens, fears, questions, petitions, and thanks to a higher being.

Kathleen Norris, in her book *Amazing Grace: A Vocabulary of Faith,* describes prayer this way: "Prayer is not doing, but being. It is not words but the beyond-words experience of coming into the presence of something much greater than oneself. It is an invitation to recognize holiness, and to utter simple words . . . in response."[4]

In this way, prayer is like mindfulness. Both are ways to focus and become one with the universe.

Norris goes on to say: "Prayer does not 'want.' It is ordinary experience lived with gratitude and wonder, a wonder that makes us know the smallness of oneself in an enormous and various universe."[5]

Prayer can enlarge our perspective and open us to new directions and influences. The wide variety of prayers ranges from the formal to personal expressions of joy, thanksgiving, and need.

To get a deeper sense of prayer, we interviewed Holly Phillips, a youth minister in Boulder, Colorado; Alan Bray, a pastor in St. Peter, Minnesota; and Rabbi Simeon Glaser of Minneapolis, Minnesota. In response to the question, "How do we [adults] give young people an understanding of prayer?," they all said that building relationships is key: spending time with young people, sharing lives with them, listening to them, and asking questions to start a discussion.

"I believe it's important to be nonjudgmental when listening to kids talk about things," said Pastor Bray. "Connecting with God and the world necessarily involves being connected with each other first."

"Kids like to explore relationships," said Rabbi Glaser,

---

[4]Kathleen Norris, *Amazing Grace: A Vocabulary of Faith* (New York: Riverhead Books, 1998), page 350.
[5]Ibid., page 351.

"perhaps because they see themselves in their relationships with others. I seek the relationship issues within the Torah as a means of gaining their interest."

In response to the question, "How can the average adult model the practice of prayer so that young people will incorporate prayer as a source of strength and inspiration?," all three all agreed that personal practice comes first, and that by sharing their prayer lives with children and youth, adults can encourage lifelong patterns of prayer. According to Holly, "It's about sharing ways to have a relationship with God through prayer." She went on to say, "Prayer can be a very personal or a public thing. Either way it is acknowledging pieces of oneself that maybe a teenager cannot acknowledge to anyone else. It is in talking through things that young people become more aware of themselves."

"Kids know a phony, so it's important to 'walk the walk,'" emphasized Rabbi Glaser. "Don't drop them at Sunday school and then go read the morning paper at the local coffeehouse. Come in with them, attend a men's club meeting, or join an adult discussion group. Let your kids know when you will be attending a meeting or education group at your synagogue. Demonstrate that your religious faith is important to you."

"Generally speaking," said Pastor Bray, "if a young person has a sense that God is in relationship and ready for a conversation 24/7, it will provide an anchor, a point of reference, a safety blanket, a rock of Gibraltar that will give confidence and hope throughout the day."

Modeling the use of prayer in life as a source of strength and inspiration keeps both young people and adults doing the often hard work of leadership.

Crafts

While it seems unusual to think of crafts as offering space for thought and meditation, such activities can become just that. Called by some the "new yoga," knitting, according to Jackie, can be a form of meditation, a spiritual connection, an opportunity to be self-reflective, and more. The physical rhythm, she says, is extremely relaxing. It is a means of gaining inner fulfillment and actually induces a meditative state.

Knitting, or a similar craft, can be especially helpful to task-oriented young people. According to Donna, knitting helped her daughter heal when she was incapacitated with a life-threatening illness. "It took her mind off her health," said Donna, "and allowed her to focus on something positive. In just one month, Heather knit twelve scarves. That year everyone in the family and all of Heather's friends received scarves for the holidays!

"Knitting just feels good," Jackie reported. "In our fast-paced world, simply doing something because it feels good and brings you pleasure is vital."

The young people at the Afrocentric Educational Academy learned about an African American tradition—story quilts—and decided that making some quilts would be a cool thing to do. A core group of four boys and two girls learned the necessary sewing skills, and, at the suggestion of their adviser, Anne Parish, they thought about ways to send a message to the people who would receive the quilts. With this suggestion in mind, the group used quilt collages that represented their thoughts and beliefs: messages of peace, love, and strengths. In all, they made five quilts to contribute to a battered women's shelter and a homeless shelter.

In creating their quilts, the young people developed communication skills, technical knowledge, and problem-solving skills. They explored community issues (domestic abuse and homelessness) and developed relationships, not only with each other and their adviser, but also with the community volunteers who assisted with the project. They learned that by giving of themselves, they connected to the larger community.

As adults we can encourage youth to knit, quilt, or try some other disciplined craft, either by teaching them the skill or learning it with them. Crafting offers a place to hear and give attention to what's in your heart and soul, and it can be a place of rest and thought. "Whatever you choose to do," Jackie suggested, "you will enhance your ability to live a creative life." Together you might get your best thinking done and emerge renewed, refreshed, and reenergized. Ultimately, crafting is about connection to yourself, the world, and others.

Above all, when we encourage young people to do "inner work," we demonstrate that we value them as individual beings, not just for what they do. As leaders who have internal skills as well as technical skills, they will be more likely to be successful in their relationships with others.

Reflections—Your Thoughts and Inspirations

Taking time to reflect on our experiences deepens our learning. It fosters critical thinking and analysis. Use the following suggestions to gain new insight into your own experiences, articulate them in writing, and apply that awareness to connect more effectively with young people.

1. What experiences did you have as a youth that gave you "space" to practice the qualities that encouraged your leadership?

   _____

   _____

   _____

   _____

   _____

2. Do you actively practice any of the personal space practices such as meditation, prayer, Tai Chi, and journaling? How has this practice made a difference in your life? How can you share this practice with others?

   _____

   _____

   _____

_____

_____

3. Think about how you claim space for yourself. When is your quiet time? Do you regularly make space in your day for it? Do you have a particular place for peacefulness and reflection? If you don't, how can you begin to make space for peacefulness and reflection?

_____

_____

_____

_____

_____

4. What do you think former Minnesota senator Paul Wellstone meant when he said, "Never separate the life you live from the words you speak"? What examples can you give from your own life about the integration of your life and speech?

_____

_____

_____

_____

_____

5. Did you ever write anything in a journal or diary or school writing project that made you stop and think? How did this knowledge become a key element in your future pursuits?

_____

_____

_____

_____

_____

6. Think about the stories of the youth at MCF–Red Wing and their comments about journaling. How you can use these stories to engage your group of young people?

_____

_____

_____

_____

_____

7. How do you allow young people the space to be themselves—without expectations? How do you allow them to practice "being"?

_____

_____

_____

_____

_____

Leadership Activities—Your Actions

For each of the activities described below, determine what specific steps you will take to complete the activity, a timeline for doing so, and a statement or two about what you hope to accomplish by completing the activity. Finally, indicate what resources you'll need to make it happen.

1. Ask young people to identify and share inspirational stories. How did people's inner strength or wisdom help them overcome difficulties? What techniques were helpful to this discovery of inner strength?

Action Steps:

Timeline:

Desired Outcomes:

Resources:

2. Invite young people to think about (describe) a time when their life was filled with a true sense of purpose or meaning—a time filled with wonder or amazement. What led to those times? How can they be recreated, treasured, expanded?

Action Steps:

Timeline:

Desired Outcomes:

Resources:

3. Join your group of young people in journaling. Suggest that you all try writing before going to bed each evening. This provides a time and space, between the business of the day and sleep, to slow down to reflect on and record the events of the day. Periodically invite students to share a few of their journal entries or talk about the challenges and opportunities of keeping a journal.

Action Steps:

Timeline:

Desired Outcomes:

Resources:

4. Invite a group of students to learn something physical like knot tying, beading, knitting, crocheting, quilting, or any craft in which one can focus on what is being done right now. Talk about how a singular activity can create mindfulness.

Action Steps:

Timeline:

Desired Outcomes:

Resources:

5. Engage a group of students in a discussion of prayer. How does it play a part in their lives?

Action Steps:

Timeline:

Desired Outcomes:

Resources:

6. Take a "time-out" with a group of young people during an activity to reflect on what they've been doing. Use it as an opportunity to change negative comments to positive ones if necessary. Or simply let them sit and pay attention to their breath. Deliberately step back and hold the silence, even if you're uncomfortable doing so. Then explore what group members perceived as the benefits/challenges of the experience.

Action Steps:

Timeline:

Desired Outcomes:

Resources:

Actions—Your Afterthoughts

After you've carried out each activity or its modification, reflect on the experience using the following guide.

1. What happened when I tried this?

_____

_____

_____

2. What did I learn?

_____

_____

_____

3. What changes will I make the next time I try it?

_____

_____

_____

4. How did these actions help young people to give voice to the leader within?

_____

_____

_____

Chapter Five

Resources

Ensuring the Capacity to Grow

Resources to help engage youth in giving voice to the leader within come in a multitude of forms: guides to service projects; stipends; release time from work or school; scholarships, transportation, meals, or snacks; connections to community organizations and their resources; training; and so forth. Youth themselves are among the greatest resources. They know and understand their needs and wants. Oftentimes, however, it takes caring, listening adults to help stimulate the action required.

At the Minnesota Alliance with Youth State Summit in November of 2004, youth were provided a booklet titled *Notebook of an Activist*. This little publication is a great guide for youth to use in planning a service project for their organization or community. It opens with the statement: "This is an issue I want to do something about in my community."

Once the issue is identified, young people are asked, "What do I know about the issue?" (the facts, the experiences, the stories). This is followed by the questions, "What do I care about and why? What is my goal?" The final question is, "Do I know others who care about the same thing?"

Once the responses to these questions are clear, the young people go on to ask another series of questions:

- Who can advise me on this issue?
- What can I do, personally, to help?
- Where can I find the resources to make it happen?

- Who can support my efforts (individuals, organizations, and so forth)?
- Where else can I go to learn more?

Adults can pull together groups of young people to explore issues suggested by this resource. For example, using the preceding format, they can explore new ways to find opportunities and space for youth to develop their "leadership voice." This process helps us teach youth to ask strategic questions and gives us the opportunity to provide honest answers or the resources to find the answers young people seek.

Once the experience is complete, we can provide space for youth to reflect on the importance of their new knowledge, skills, and experiences. During this structured time, they can also reflect on the impact of their efforts in the community, on the people they served, on the system, and on themselves.

Because young people come to us with different levels of experience and resources, we are continually challenged to find projects and experiences that serve as equalizers. Providing time for them to identify the issues and then partnering them with like-minded individuals and resources is an effective method. To be truly inclusive calls on us to be both creative and open-minded.

Transportation

Transportation is one of the biggest barriers to volunteer and leadership involvement. Parents work, bus service isn't always available, and some students are too young to drive. Everything else that we talk about in this book goes out the window unless we are able to provide safe, reliable transportation for young people. It's about creating mechanisms to ensure authentic involvement, or, as some would say, meaningful participation, across the spectrum!

While involved in VOICE (Voicing Our Intelligence to Challenge Education) at his high school, Via had to find transportation to and from meetings. His parents didn't drive, and neither did he. Unless he could catch a ride with friends, he spent an extraordinary amount of time either walking or taking the city bus. The transportation issue was solved when the adult coordinator provided the ride. Of even greater value than the transportation were the socializing conversations that occurred between Via and the coordinator during the comings and goings. The time together provided a level playing field, filled with trust and respect, between Via and the coordinator.

If the leaders of an organization cannot provide transportation, they need to secure it by offering mileage reimbursements to students or their parents, bus tokens, or taxi fare. Some organizations like Phillips Community TV, an out-of-school program in the media arts, purchased a van and drivers' insurance to bring young participants from school to the community center. Other organizations have hired private drivers when that is the only option.

When parents drive their young people to an event, invite them in to observe—but not to participate. When parents observe, they gain a different type of understanding and involvement with their children that can bring added value to family conversations.

When faced with transportation issues, young people can brainstorm options and determine what works best for them. They can then assume responsibility for their individual choices.

Connections

Although on some days it may seem hard to believe, young people do want adults in their lives. They are hungry for connections with adults they can trust. And as they struggle to stretch their wings of independence, they want to be connected to caring adults who also respect and value them.

In a Hennepin County (Minnesota) youth development and community mapping project conducted by youth and adults in several neighborhoods in the Twin Cities, researchers discovered that two of the greatest needs were (1) increased adult involvement in the lives of youth and (2) more programs that helped youth participate in the larger world, especially those that exposed them to careers and opportunities outside of their neighborhoods.

> *Although on some days it may seem hard to believe, young people do want adults in their lives.*

Some young people have to overcome obstacles to other types of connections. If they don't have access to the Internet, for example, you can arrange a connection through a public library or other institution. If parents aren't sure about their child's involvement in a particular activity, you can visit with them to explore their concerns and gain their trust. Knowing their child has more than one advocate is so encouraging to parents!

Whatever the case, engaging young people in making connections and overcoming obstacles pays dividends for them—and for everyone. In their "Connecting Is Key" campaign, Callie and Will said this about making connections across generations: "Our greatest hope is that each of us—youth and adults—continue to reach out to all youth, especially the unconnected, and make a connection. Give them a chance. Create leadership opportunities with them. Trust them, support them, enjoy them, respect them. The results will be spectacular."

Callie and Will outline four key concepts in creating those connections:

- Respect: Because we are each of equal value.
- Trust: Because we need each other.
- Responsibility: Because who else will do it?
- Partnership: Because we benefit from each other's ideas.

Scholarships

Scholarships for young people to attend conferences, seminars, and training sessions are critical for their development as leaders. Many young people, especially those in disadvantaged families, simply don't have the means to pay registration costs, and local organizations are often strapped for funds.

Search Institute, for example, raises money for scholarships so that a large number of youth, as well as adults, can attend its national conference. In fact, its annual goal for conference fund-raising is equal parts conference support and scholarships.

The peace education and service organization youthrive will not turn students away from its gatherings for lack of funds. Staff and volunteers (both youth and adults) raise the necessary fees to accommodate all who want to attend by sending out appeal letters, hosting fund-raising events, and including a line item for scholarships in their proposals.

Individuals, as well as organizations and businesses, are also a good source of scholarship funds—especially older citizens who recognize the opportunity to give back in ways that will enhance the development of young leaders. In many cases, all you have to do is ask. And ask you must, as potential contributors may not be aware of the opportunities you are providing for youth.

Youth are great partners in raising scholarship funds as well as program dollars. With a little training, coaching, and support, they make excellent spokespersons. Contributors respond positively to having young people involved! In addition to helping "make the ask," they practice leadership by participating in the planning and the appropriate follow-up. Young people also excel in creating and conducting car washes, yard services, bake sales, house cleaning, dog walking, silent auctions, garage sales, and other fund-raising events. Adults partnered with youthrive young leaders developing, designing, and producing products to sell online and in catalogs to promote peace building and raise funds to support their leadership activities. In doing so, they exercise a variety of leadership skills and build impressive résumés that can make a difference on scholarship applications.

Most important, young people want to be viewed as part of the solution.

Most important, young people want to be viewed as part of the solution. Therefore, your expectation that they will be involved in helping to raise scholarship funds for various conferences and trainings is viewed with respect and appreciation. As the founder of Citizens' Scholarship Foundation of America, Irving A. Fradkin, was fond of saying, "We're offering students a hand up, not a handout."

Paid Expenses, Release Time, and Other Incentives

Offering stipends to help pay expenses for their participation in focus groups and community organizations often provides a "hook" to get young people interested in leadership work. It also demonstrates respect for their time. Most often, once they see what's involved, young people come back for more.

In the pilot "Summer of Peace" program in the Folwell neighborhood of Minneapolis, middle school students were invited to take an eight-week course with peace-related activities: all participants were paid $150. At the end of the eight weeks, one of the coordinators asked a student why he had taken part. "For the money, of course," he responded boldly. When she pointed out to him that at forty hours a week for eight weeks, he wasn't even making fifty cents an hour, he grinned up at her and said, "I really liked it, too. It was cool!"

Stipends are also important because some young people are taking care of younger brothers and sisters or have to work to help their families. Some have children themselves. Remember, the goal should be to ensure that all young people can be involved. Paying for expenses makes opportunities for everyone, not just those who can afford to participate.

Young people who are holding down jobs can, with the support of adults, talk to their employers to arrange "release time" to participate in community leadership events. Today many companies recognize the strategic advantages of employee community involvement. It enhances a company's reputation and image in the community, builds goodwill, and expands the business's network, markets, and access to key customer groups. Community involvement by employees expands the opportunities for them to acquire leadership and management skills important to the workplace. In addition to increasing a company's ability to attract potential employees by positioning itself as a great place to work, employee involvement in meaningful community service can also enhance employee motivation, morale, loyalty, and retention.

Companies may also be willing to provide "gift cards" that can be used by the young leaders' families as a reward for service in the community.

If your leadership opportunity occurs during the school day, you can work with school staff to arrange for class credit. Another incentive is to offer mileage reimbursement for young people or their parents to bring them to events. Providing funds for taxis and buses is another option.

As part of the creative process for developing ScholarShop®, a curriculum designed to motivate and prepare young people for postsecondary education, Marlys offered small stipends for youth to come to focus groups to share their ideas and concerns about college. In addition to content, she asked them to respond to format, design, and color. They were thrilled and proud to be included in such an important project. Once the draft was completed, she reconvened the group to get feedback. Participants were amazed to see their ideas incorporated into the program. It was a confidence-building leadership experience!

In cases where young people don't feel they need or want to accept a stipend, suggest arrangements for contributing the funds to a charity of their choice. This gives them an opportunity to give, as well as receive, and an understanding of philanthropy.

Meals

Making a simple meal together with young people creates harmony and responsibility. Sitting down to share that meal provides a relaxed atmosphere in which students can share their lives. Eating and talking together as equals is a relationship builder that strengthens the whole group process. It is a sign of respect.

Sharing a meal in an ethnic restaurant offers youth several opportunities. It can be a time to broaden their knowledge of other cultures and other types of food. Hosting a meeting in various communities becomes an adventure and puts kids on an equal footing with each other. Young people can take turns doing the research, selecting the restaurant, and recommending various foods on the menu. A way to deepen the learning that takes place in these types of situations is to prepare meals from different ethnic traditions as a group and have the young people teach each other about their respective cultures.

Lunch in a coffee shop outside the neighborhood offers opportunities to learn about products (e.g., free-trade coffee), cultures, and consumerism. Eating out can be a springboard for a discussion about nutrition, exercise, and careers in the restaurant business.

These suggestions illustrate why including food in project budgets is so critical. While eating is important to young people, the cross-cultural experience is just as crucial as the food. Another important factor is the going to and coming from. "I have some of my best conversations with young people in the car," Donna said. And if you have a group in the car, they begin to build a bond with each other. By using every chance to deepen the experience and the relationships, you connect young people with each other and with the world around them.

> *"I have some of my best conversations with young people in the car."*

Training

Young people soak up knowledge and experiences. "I see myself in a role that will allow for endless exploration of new concepts and ideas," said Callie. "I am involved in an ongoing search for exciting opportunities that allow me to discover more about myself as a leader. And I do not see that search ending in five to ten years but continuing my whole life through."

Samantha was thrilled by the opportunity to go to a youth leadership camp. There she met students from diverse communities and learned a variety of skills that she put to use once she returned home. "I was interested to learn," she observed, "that despite our different origins, what teens think about is usually the same."

In scouting out appropriate training resources, look for ones that build on the experiences young people already have, not just those that are youth-related. And prepare participants before they go: What should they take along? What should they wear? How do they decide on what sessions to attend if it is a large conference rather than a specific training? How do they take notes? What are your expectations for their sharing what they learned?

After they return home, work with participants to demonstrate specific skill-building activities based on their new knowledge. Teaching others reinforces new capabilities and perspectives. Arrange opportunities for them to make presentations to groups of adults, especially those who may have supported the experience.

If you are the one offering training or facilitating a meeting, set aside time after the gathering to spend time with the young people. Responding to their questions is one thing. Actually engaging them in conversation is even better. By doing so, you demonstrate that you care about them and that you value their time as well as what they have to say. The conversation takes you out of the "expert" mode and is one more way to establish equitable roles.

Playing the Numbers Game: Relationship Resources

A number of resources are available that offer youth and adults guidelines, examples, and inspiration for building lasting, meaningful relationships and leadership capabilities. Rather than delve into details about each of these frameworks and programs, we simply list them here and encourage our readers to go to the respective Web sites for specific information and additional resources, both in print and online.

Another option is to use a search engine to explore topics such as youth leadership, positive youth development, adolescent brain development, youth service, and youth activism:

- 40 Developmental Assets® Framework of Search Institute: www.search-institute.org
- 4-H Youth Program Resources: www.national4-hheadquarters.org
- Five Promises of America's Promise: www.americaspromise.org
- *The 7 Habits of Highly Effective Teens* by Sean Covey: a popular, widely available book based on the writing of Stephen R. Covey, Sean's father
- Six Pillars of Character: www.charactercounts.org

Beyond "the numbers," a variety of organizations are available for students who are interested in expanding their leadership through volunteer opportunities:

- AmeriCorps: www.americorps.org
- Corporation for National and Community Service: www.nationalservice.gov
- Do Something: www.dosomething.org
- Family, Career and Community Leaders of America, Inc.: www.fcclainc.org
- Hands on Network: www.handsonnetwork.org
- Kids Voting USA: www.kidsvotingusa.com
- Konopka Institute for Best Practices in Adolescent Health: www.konopka.umn.edu
- Mentor: www.mentoring.org
- Minnesota Association for Children's Mental Health: www.macmh.org

- Minnesota Human Rights Education Experience: www.thisismyhome.org
- National Youth Leadership Council: www.nylc.org
- Points of Light Foundation: www.pointsoflight.org
- Yo' the Movement: www.yothemovement.org
- Youth on Board: www.youthonboard.org
- Youth Service America: www.servenet.org and www.ysa.org
- PeaceJam Foundation: www.peacejam.org
- What Kids Can Do: www.whatkidscando.org
- youthrive: www.youthrive.net

If you are interested in providing resources on giving to satisfy community needs, check out www.learningtogive.org.

Overcoming Challenges and Obstacles

Often the single most essential element in becoming a leader is confidence. And becoming self-confident is a huge challenge to young people.

Will shared this story: "I remember sitting in conference rooms with people who have professional titles longer than the alphabet seemed able to support. Initially, I just listened and said little. But I began to see these perfectly capable people suggest things and get excited about ideas that the rest of the room simply ignored. I began to think—well if these people can be off target, can suggest crazy things, what harm can come from my throwing in my two cents. It goes back to not being afraid to say, 'I don't know,' and letting a young person know his/her idea is at least as good as everyone else's. In school, among peers, this idea comes more naturally—everyone is at the same level of education and age. In other circumstances, this isn't so obvious."

Challenges and obstacles help young people to hone their leadership skills. Sometimes they have to overcome people telling them that "it doesn't make a difference." That's the challenge that propelled Erko. At first, he felt it wasn't his place to stand up and say or do something. Once he started to get involved, he had to ignore continual putdowns. However, he said, "As time went on, I saw that my actions did make a difference, and that it was *my place* to try to make a difference, regardless of what other people might say."

Often young people have to overcome critical, rather than positive, feedback. This is especially difficult when they have fragile images of themselves to begin with, or they are taking on a new area. We can help young people face these challenges in a variety of ways.

First, we can engage them in envisioning what it might be like beforehand and reflecting after the challenge has been met or not met.

Second, we can review with them a variety of options and guide the process of finding solutions or a way around the challenge. We can also explore with them how a solution or response in one activity can be transferred to another. Then we can explore with them the differences and similarities of the activities, always giving them the space to think it through.

Third, we can help young people look more broadly at what might build on their talents and skills, then guide them in prioritizing and finding a balance in their lives. So many youth are faced with a multitude of activities and responsibilities that you wonder how they have time to sleep, much less eat

Too often, young people feel overwhelmed. Truly, they simply need time to be.

or dream a little. Finding a balance among sports, school, family, friends, work, leadership opportunities in the community, and faith-based activities is difficult. Too often, young people feel overwhelmed. Truly, they simply need time *to be.*

We can help young people see that while all of these aspects of their lives are important, family and school come first. Their other involvements need to enhance their lives, not burden them.

Fourth, we might also illustrate how to "hand off" responsibilities—to delegate to others when they are feeling stressed. We want to explore options for handling their involvement in such a way that they won't think they have failed us in not getting it all done. If we have built trust and respect with young people, they will feel comfortable in letting us know when the experience becomes a burden.

These four methods for meeting challenges offer paths to a lifelong healthy lifestyle.

Coaching

Personal coaching is about unlocking a person's potential to maximize her or his own performance. As a resource, personal coaches establish an ongoing inquiry process for youth to create their own solutions, as opposed to imparting expertise, knowledge, or recommendations. They also provide encouragement and accountability for action. As a result, young people gain in self-awareness. They become tuned in to their own unique strengths and talents.

In Jackie's words, "We humans are like an acorn that contains within it all the potential to be a magnificent oak tree. We need nourishment, encouragement, and the light to reach toward, but the 'oak-treeness' is already within. Personal coaching helps young people discover this 'oak-treeness'!"

A variety of benefits accrue to young people through personal coaching: a greater ability to think for themselves, greater awareness of all things that enhance performance, enjoyment, a greater sense of responsibility, an enhanced self-belief, and an understanding of how to self-coach.

As an experienced personal coach, Jackie believes that open-ended questions are the most effective means for generating awareness and responsibility.

Adults who may not have formal training as coaches can still help young people by developing their own capacities for the following skills:

- Listening for the theme that will intensify the learning—for the vision, values, and purpose expressed.
- Using our intuition—synthesizing impressions and information.
- Being curious—open, inviting, spacious, almost playful. Curiosity frames the question-asking process.
- Promoting active learning—not explaining or informing or entertaining but rather advancing a course of action and intensifying the learning.

As adults, we can become coaches to youth by being totally (but respectfully) curious about their dreams and aspirations, about what makes them tick, about their values, and how they live their values. We can encourage them to clarify their goals and provide the tools for action and learning that lead to the results they seek. We can ask the powerful questions that help youth seek their own answers. And we should do all of this without judgment, without analyzing, only with acceptance.

Family

As mentioned in other chapters, family is very important to most young people. Many Millennials view their parents as their best friends.

The young people we interviewed are no exceptions. For the most part, their parents push them to be their best and tell them that what they do is fantastic. Often the parents join with their sons and daughters as volunteers. Mike said his parents were the best volunteers he could ask for when trying to accomplish a project. Will's parents supported him by recognizing that his out-of-school commitments were valuable.

And finally, Callie's family inspired her to be a leader by expressing their pride in what she did. And through her own leadership, she was able to change her grandfather's opinion of her generation. She tells this story: "Upon returning from a youth trip to Washington, D.C., my grandfather admitted to me that he had more or less given up on Generation Y [another name for the Millennials]. He assumed the primary concern of youth was TV and video games. My trip to D.C. made him realize that youth are very interested in what is going on in the world. Youth are not afraid to challenge the policies and rules [set forth by adults] that affect them. The influence my leadership had on my grandfather's opinion of Generation Y is possibly one of my greatest personal accomplishments."

Parents can engage children of all ages in taking leadership responsibility in planning and implementing family projects, activities, and volunteering. One of the great teaching opportunities comes when the family, together, researches the systemic reasons for their support of a particular cause. It allows them to look at the broader issues of justice, poverty, peace, and so forth.

Perhaps most crucial is to be there when they need you, no matter the time or your own commitments.

Perhaps most crucial is to be there when they need you, no matter the time or your own commitments. If they call or wake you at 2 A.M. to talk, be there for them. Be in the moment with them, for that's when you'll see and hear what is truly important to them.

Of course, not all young people have supportive families. In these cases, we must use our own best judgment about the depth of involvement and responsibility we want to take for individual young people, keeping in mind that they especially need our support and trust. Finding opportunities and resources for their equal participation is critical and oh, so rewarding!

Reflections—Your Thoughts and Inspirations

Taking time to reflect on our experiences deepens our learning. It fosters critical thinking and analysis. Use the following suggestions to gain new insight into your own experiences, articulate them in writing, and apply that awareness to connect more effectively with young people.

1. As a young person, did you attend a camp, retreat, seminar, or conference? What resources made it possible for you to attend? What leadership skills came as a result of your attendance?

_____

_____

_____

_____

_____

2. Think about a time when you were young, and an adult in your life connected you to an opportunity or person who helped you accomplish a goal or change your life in some way. How did this assistance make you feel? What difference did it make? How can you provide this help for someone else?

_____

_____

_____

_____

_____

3. What challenges and obstacles did you have to overcome as a young person? How did that affect who you are today? How are current challenges and obstacles different from or similar to the ones you faced when you were young?

_____

_____

_____

_____

_____

4. Think back to a time when you missed an opportunity because you didn't have the resources. What would have happened if you had been able to be engaged? Who might have stepped up to the plate but didn't?

_____

_____

_____

_____

_____

5. Recall a time when you spent quality time with someone in your family. What did you learn? How did you feel? How might you provide, in this busy world, quality time for a member of your family or someone in your neighborhood, workplace, or place of worship?

_____

_____

_____

_____

_____

Leadership Activities—Your Actions

For each of the activities described below, determine what specific steps you will take to complete the activity, a timeline for doing so, and a statement or two about what you hope to accomplish by completing the activity. Finally, indicate what resources you'll need to make it happen.

1. What young people do you know who could benefit from attending a particular conference, seminar, or training. How could you make that happen? What resources can you provide? Whom else can you approach for help?

Action Steps:

Timeline:

Desired Outcomes:

Resources:

2. Young people appreciate being asked for their ideas and opinions. Think about the community or faith-based organizations to which you are connected. What issue or topic would benefit from a youth voice or perspective? Convene a focus group of six to ten young people—keeping in mind the ground rules for such an activity—and learn from them.[1] If possible, offer a stipend for their time.

Action Steps:

---

[1]Ground rules for focus groups and group discussions:
- All ideas are good ideas.
- No judgment.
- Listen to each other
- It's OK to disagree.
- One conversation at a time.
- Have fun.

Timeline:

Desired Outcomes:

Resources:

3. Work with your group of young people to create a talents and gifts bank or a resource network through which youth can share their talents with each other. How could this "bank" be helpful to other groups in the community? With your youth, explore the benefits derived from this type of project for them, each other, and the community.

Action Steps:

Timeline:

Desired Outcomes:

Resources:

4. Host a meeting with youth at an ethnic restaurant in your community. Or visit a farmers' market to explore with vendors different foods and cultures. What does "organic" mean? What are the growing times needed for various kinds of produce? How do you move products to market? What is fair trade? What are sustainable resources? Ask the provocative question, "What is your energy footprint?" Talk with young people about the ways they can broaden their knowledge of the world around them.

Action Steps:

Timeline:

Desired Outcomes:

Resources:

5. Invite young people together to chronicle their volunteer and leadership experiences in a journal or a one-page essay that can be used to complete scholarship and college applications. Use this time to explore existing leadership conferences and other conferences and learning activities to expand their résumés.

Action Steps:

_____

Timeline:

_____

Desired Outcomes:

_____

Resources:

_____

Actions—Your Afterthoughts

After you've carried out each activity or its modification, reflect on the experience using the following guide.

1. What happened when I tried this?

_____

_____

_____

2. What did I learn?

_____

_____

_____

3. What changes will I make the next time I try it?

_____

_____

_____

4. How did these actions help young people to give voice to the leader within?

_____

_____

_____

Chapter Six

Outcomes

Encouraging a New Generation of Leaders

What can you expect if you take time to provide the support, opportunities, space, and resources to the young people within your sphere of influence? You can expect personal growth and greater influence! You can see change unfold. And you can expect young people to know that they are making a difference! They grow to understand that leaders make change happen.

"My work just didn't help my friends and family," said Via, "but also my own life. I came to realize that I could do anything if I just try. I am most impressed with the positive things I do. Most of all, I feel good when I know that I've made a positive influence on my friends."

Increased Self-Confidence and Confidence in the World around Them

When young leaders discover the leadership voice within, it is often a transformational experience. They gain the assurance and the knowledge that they have the *power* to lead and that this power will help them transform their schools, places of worship, communities, and the world. This confidence also opens them to others, including adults. They feel fully alive, living a life of purpose and fulfillment! As effective leaders they feel successful.

Through their leadership, young people learn how to cope with a wide variety of problems and a wide variety of people. As a result, they feel they've made an impact, and they express heightened satisfaction and confidence in their lives at work, at school, and at home.

Gaining self-possession, understanding how they affect others, discerning their strengths and what works are all outcomes of leadership experiences. Learning how to ask for help and managing responsibility and authority also result in self-confidence. Sharing their own vision for a project and gathering input and support for the project are just two ways they gain confidence in the people and communities in which they live.

Even projects that don't work out can strengthen self-confidence and self-efficacy skills. For example, when young people create a fund-raiser, and not enough people show up to raise the money they envisioned, take time to explore the possible reasons and what could have been done differently. Recognize that not meeting the financial goal isn't the only thing that disappoints. It's also the fact that not enough people supported them in their efforts. Reflect on the variables that affected the project and plan for what can be done differently on the next project. Celebrate your working and learning together.

The involvement in an organization can also change a young person's perspective of self. Chris came from an abusive home. His parents moved from place to place because his dad wouldn't pay taxes, so when collectors started coming around, they moved. Chris had no friends. Then he became involved in El Pamar, a youth-driven organization that makes determinations on grants for nonprofits. The next time his family moved, Chris refused to go with them. A teacher living nearby took Chris into her home. He has received college scholarships and is in his final years of engineering school. He said of his involvement in El Pamar, "I thought I had it tough until I realized so many are far worse off. Even without my family, I can count on my friends, teachers, and myself."

Commitment to Lifelong Leadership

In our minds, Maya exemplifies commitment to lifelong leadership. "I think power and leadership contribute to commitment," she said. "You become used to being able to get things done, being able to call for meetings, and talk to people directly to move things. I think, too, that once you have a position of leadership, and you learn from that experience and (hopefully) reflect on what went well, and what you may have handled in another way, you can more easily approach future leadership responsibilities."

When asked how leadership had transformed her life, Maya responded: "It has transformed my life in many wonderful ways. First, it has made me more 'on top of things'—having responsibility and knowing that how a group does will ultimately make me look good or look foolish, I've had to manage a lot of parts of my life (school, friends, etc.) to give myself ample time to manage my service responsibilities effectively.

"Second, I think these experiences have increased my self-confidence. For example, when I was lead Promise Fellow at the University of Minnesota during my freshman year, I managed the other fifteen undergrad and grad Promise Fellows on campus. While I had a great deal of experience with America's Promise and was probably the most qualified for the job, some of the fellows didn't exactly appreciate that, considering my age. One of the grad student Promise Fellows would not respond to my e-mails or voice-mails. That was a challenge because he knew that I knew America's Promise, and he didn't. Working through that situation, and now looking back, I feel like I can handle skepticism about my age or other facets of my being more effectively than if I had not experienced this situation. I guess I really am committed to making a difference!"

Saying No to Negative Choices

According to Heather, one of the most important things we can do to help young people say no to negative choices is to make the positive choice more attractive, interesting, and exciting. Most young people love a sense of adventure! We need to make them want to come, to try the positive choice. And we can do this by offering challenging opportunities, stipends, scholarships, transportation, food, fun, and so forth (see chapter 5 on resources). Sharing our own joyful spirit will also draw in young people.

During a Day of Peace at the Minnesota Correctional Facility at Red Wing (MCF-Red Wing), one of the young men involved in the day's events told another that if he had been exposed to positive ways of doing things, he never would have been incarcerated. He lacked examples and experiences that many other young people had. No one in his life had offered him a different way to think about his behavior until he heard a Tibetan monk describe his own capture and torture by the Chinese when they invaded his homeland.

In the monk's story, the young offender found a different way to think about his own life. The monk at first feared that he would lose his compassion because of the torture. Instead, he discovered deeper compassion. The young man saw, through the monk's story, that he clearly had other choices—that options for peace and compassion, not just violence and anger, did exist!

While we may never know for sure, we trust that the young man who had this experience will be able to say no to negative choices in the future because he saw how strong positive options could be.

The Ability to Work Cooperatively

Most young people today have plenty of ways to be engaged competitively through sports, grades, and other types of contests. Through volunteering and service in the community, we can also provide uncompetitive methods that enhance young people's ability to work cooperatively.

Planning community events and community service opportunities is a natural way to build cooperation across generations. For example, in the community asset-mapping activity mentioned in chapter 3, young people were partners with adults in doing surveys and interviews as well as preparing and delivering the follow-up reports and presentations.

In developing the project "Between You and Me, Connecting Is Key," in Big Lake, Minnesota, youth reached out to the Big Lake Lions Club, which eagerly explored ideas for connecting with them. The club also provided financial resources. Youth and adults put age-based assumptions aside and gravitated to the project. As a result, they realized a new level of respect for each other and the things they could accomplish together.

The Ability to Step Out in Front, Often Alone

Stepping out beyond our comfort zone is difficult for all of us, adult or youth. It takes courage—"guts," young people would say—and if a young person decides to do so, he or she will often benefit from practicing with an adult and playing out various scenarios about potential consequences.

At a youth conference, Salina stood up and talked about her challenges with mental health issues. Her message of hope was to "reach back" to support other young people who were experiencing similar struggles. In speaking out, Salina invited audience members to look into their own issues and encouraged them to seek help to meet their challenges.

Stepping out beyond our comfort zone is difficult for all of us, adult or youth.

By sharing her own situation, Salina helped reduce the stigma and isolation that so often come with mental health issues. She demonstrated that it is okay to speak out and ask for, as well as give, support. In fact, this courageous young woman has now started a peer-to-peer group with other young people who face mental health challenges. Together they are working on an awareness campaign to change people's perceptions of mental illness and mentoring younger students faced with similar issues. By sharing their experiences, they are building personal strengths and stimulating changes in their communities. Today Salina is expanding her leadership by serving on other youth advisory groups.

Spoken-word events—poetry, storytelling, and even political or social commentary as performance—are a fairly recent phenomenon that can dramatically increase a young person's self-confidence, communication skills (both written and oral), and sense of belonging. They provide opportunities for young people from diverse cultures to express their feelings and share their life stories.

Two poets on the spoken-word circuit (coffee houses, college campuses, and community centers), Ed Bok Lee and Bao Phi, live in the Twin Cities of Minneapolis and Saint Paul. In addition to their public performances, they also conduct high school workshops. "Spoken word really addresses the struggles and issues that young people relate to," said Phi in a *Minneapolis Star Tribune* article.[1] "For a lot of kids, it's their only way to speak out."

For more information, enter "spoken word" into your computer search engine to explore a variety of associations, trainings, and spoken-word events across the country.

Change a Course of Action

Young people, given leadership experience, are able to take that experience and change a course of action, both personally and for something or someone outside themselves. When this expansion happens, it is marvelous to see.

When a new immigrant group moves into a community, the demographics change, the school population shifts, and tension between the newcomers and current residents may develop. Some groups tend to feel isolated and do not interact.

---

[1]Tom Horgan, "Wide, Wide Word," *Minneapolis Star Tribune,* May 28, 2006.

Enter onstage a leadership group of young people, including both Erko and Via, who worked with other young people to plan a cultural festival to promote understanding among the various cultural groups at school.

Individuals from each immigrant group were invited to be part of the planning and implementation of the event that included booths representative of the cultures in the school population. Culturally specific entertainment, games, and food were included. Photos documented both the process and the success of the event.

The planning and implementation of this event changed the school environment; groups started to cooperate and interact, and the enhanced relationships spilled into the community.

Initiate a Course of Action

When young leaders dedicate themselves to an organization with a mission that inspires and motivates them, they gain the knowledge and experience to set goals and objectives and look for measurable results. They value the strengths of others and know how to actively engage them in reaching the goals set for them.

When Callie and Will initiated "Connecting Is Key," and Michael designed Fast Forward, they started activities that remain alive in their communities even though they have gone off to college, careers, and new leadership roles in different organizations. Each of these young people stresses that the keys to success are a positive attitude, the belief that they could do it, and a sense of shared responsibility for everyone involved.

As just one example of such capacities in action, in several communities, groups of young people, tired of being told they could not skateboard on the sidewalks or in parking lots, have formed skateboarding clubs and, with adults as partners, developed skateboarding and bike parks.

Will's advice: "JUST START."

Influence Someone Else

Wherever a need exists, young people can help address it. Involve them as part of the solution. Identifying your impact and influence on someone is powerful. It happens often, without our knowing it, and when young people recognize their influence, it increases self-confidence and self-efficacy and contributes to the sense that they *do* make a difference.

> *Wherever a need exists, young people can help address it.*

Participating in a Day of Peace at MCF-Red Wing was as meaningful for the young people who worked to bring the event to the young residents as it was to those who were incarcerated. One of them led the peace flag activity, which allowed residents to reflect on a thought or experience that made them feel peaceful. The goal was to connect with residents and shape new life skills. At the end of the day, one young man asked how he might stay connected to PeaceJam, the event organizer. "You know," he said, "if I had been with something like this, I don't think I'd be here now." He added, somewhat regretfully, "This is the kind of thing 'good' kids get to do."

"I am still struck by the power of creating opportunities that demonstrate to young people that they are competent individuals, valuable citizens, and positive leaders," said a youth leader. "By creating opportunities for youth offenders to plan the event, by engaging them as equals, and by working with them to build skills instead of preaching, lecturing, or criticizing, *we inspired residents to believe in their potential.*"

We believe this statement says it all: by engaging youth as equals in planning, implementing, and evaluating activities, we influence their sense of well-being and competence. Reaching out in this way helps reframe how they see themselves—in this case, as leaders who will reenter their home communities as peace builders, not ex-offenders.

Community's Competitive Advantage

When youth are given opportunities to be involved in the community, they bring a competitive advantage for the community. They demonstrate that healthy, competent, and caring young people contribute to a healthy community, and a healthy community appeals to people as a good place to live, shop, and work—a good place to raise their children, a place where youth thrive and leaders guide.

When Haley and Jack's parents considered a move to a new community, the first thing they did was to visit the new school and meet with the principal and a few teachers to assess their children's opportunities for success. They were impressed, not only by the people they met, but also by the programs and a school

"I am still struck by the power of creating opportunities that demonstrate to young people that they are competent individuals, valuable citizens, and positive leaders."

climate that fostered academic as well as social growth and avenues for leadership. Students in the older grades were involved in a variety of activities through which they interacted with younger children.

To extend this reasoning—even to the point of the obvious—stronger young people create a stronger society where authentic leaders keep in mind the *common good* of all citizens.

We find that the opportunity to give voice to the leader within often reinforces young people's motivation to do well in school and stay engaged in service to their communities. Regardless of background, once young people have the chance to exercise leadership, they begin to excel in other ways.

Where Youth Leaders See Themselves in Five to Ten Years Demonstrates Outcomes

Young people, particularly those who are marginalized, have a hard time connecting themselves to the future. The young people to whom Jackie posed the question of envisioning their future all said they could not see that far. Most were looking at college as their future, and beyond was an unknown.

However, at least one of the youth leaders we interviewed was very clear about his expectations for himself. In five years, Michael saw himself completing an undergraduate degree in economics and international management. In ten years, he would be doing two things: running his own company and working for the United Nations. "I don't know how yet," he said, "but the desire is there. And when I have the desire, I can make it happen."

"I don't know where I'll be in ten years," Maya responded. "I am open and flexible to signs and paths that might open." In this respect, she was like Mike, who was not sure where life would take him beyond college. "I sometimes think it is better this way than setting definite plans," he said.

Today we know that their commitment to attend college contributed to longer-term career decisions. Maya is in both medical and business school, and Mike is in law school. While these career directions have been decided, they are both open to where this educational background will lead them. As young people have more experiences, their career paths change as more possibilities open for them.

Surveys

Although the preceding examples prove the effectiveness of encouraging young people to give voice to the leader within, research evidence also supports this critical activity. In a paper titled "The Contribution of Community Service and Service-Learning to Academic Achievement among Socioeconomically Disadvantaged Students," researchers report that students with higher levels of service and service-learning indicated higher grades, attendance, and other academic success outcomes.[2] In

---

[2]P. C. Scales, E. C. Roehlkepartain, M. Neal, J. C. Kielsmier, and P. L. Benson (in press), "The Contribution of Community Service and Service-Learning to Academic Achievement among Socioeconomically Disadvantaged Students," *Journal of Experiential Education.*

another study, students who reported "greater connection to community" in middle school, including participating in community service, youth programs, and religious community, were three times more likely than others to have a B+ or higher average three years later in high school.[3] Additionally, Search Institute reports that an "analyses of the aggregate dataset of 217,000 students found that students who reported serving others at least one hour per week were significantly less likely to report school problems (poor attendance and below average grades) and significantly more likely to report school success (self-report of earning mostly As in school) than those who did not service others at least one hour per week."[4]

"And when I have the desire, I can make it happen."

In the 1996 Independent Sector/Gallup Poll, youth reported the top ten benefits of volunteering:

- They learned to respect others.
- They learned to be helpful and kind.
- They learned how to get along with and relate to others.
- They gained satisfaction from helping others.
- They learned to understand people who were different from themselves.
- They learned how to relate to younger children.
- They became better people.
- They learned new skills.
- They developed leadership skills.
- They became more patient with others.

In 2005, the Corporation for National and Community Service partnered with Independent Sector and the U.S. Census

---

[3]P. C. Scales, P. L. Benson A. Sesma Jr., E. C. Roehlkepartain, and M. van Dulmen (in press), "The Role of Developmental Assets in Predicting Academic Achievement: A Longitudinal Study," *Journal of Adolescence*.

[4]P. C. Scales and E. C. Roehlkepartain, "Service to Others: A Gateway Asset for School Success and Healthy Development," Growing to Greatness, 2004, National Youth Leadership Council.

Bureau in a major federal survey of youth volunteering. The following are key findings from this survey:

- Fifty-five percent of youth volunteer.
- Three-fourths of youth who volunteer do so through religious, school, or youth organizations.
- Youth volunteers do better in school than their classmates who don't volunteer.
- If family members volunteer, young people will, too.
- Religious attendance has a strong link to youth volunteering.

Outcomes for Adults

Giving voice to the leader within brings benefits for young people. Just as important, being involved with youth results in terrific benefits for adults. We continue to learn and grow from shared wisdom, and we view the world and its concerns in new and fresh ways. We can look at serious issues and have fun at the same time! Donna said, "As a result of my connection with young people, I feel things more deeply and often wear those feelings on my sleeve!"

Being involved with youth results in terrific benefits for adults.

The most common response to our question regarding benefits to adults who work with young people echoes the remarks of Abdul Mohamed, who works with Somali youth and their parents in St. Paul, Minnesota. "When they [youth] do better and succeed, I feel great!" he said in a recent interview. "I treat them as an equal human being, and I get the same respect in return."

According to Holly Phillips, the youth minister in Boulder, Colorado, young people are reflecting God's light by doing many wonderful things in their lives and communities, but we simply are not focused on those positive aspects of their behavior. "Given our society," she wrote, "we hear about the best and the catastrophes but not always the everyday ways in which some of the most amazing things are happening."

"I benefit each and every day by our youth," Holly added. "I have the delight of watching the most changeable people in the world, children and youth. As they have epiphanies, as they begin to understand and relate to God and each other, I am overjoyed! This gives me much hope for our world. They also challenge me to change and be transformed. Our young people have taught me about the face of God and what he looks like in each person."

Nicky Metchnek, a school social worker, also finds joy in working with young people. "The joy that comes to me is knowing that I've helped them grow and that they are better equipped to meet the world head-on," she said.

Young people also can make adults feel younger, more joyful, and more active. They are a reminder that having fun is a necessary part of life. "Kids let me know that making good decisions is an important thing to learn and remember," said Pastor Bray. "Watching kids make mistakes has reminded me to be a little gentler and forgiving of myself—we're all still learning how to live a good life, how to love people as we've been loved by God, how to find contentment in little things. Young people tend to blow the lid off pretense, hypocrisy, and posturing—I have benefited from that reminder, too. They keep us attuned to those things which are basic. I need that."

Rabbi Glaser reported that he benefited from the "extraordinary and fulfilling" responses of young people to him as a person. "Kids are a barometer to how we are doing," Rabbi Glaser said.

Lessons Learned

As we mentioned in the introduction, an early reviewer of our manuscript said that "it's almost too positive." She asked if there ever was something we tried that didn't work. And if so, what had we learned from it that we could share?

Far from having perfect experiences, we readily admit that working with young people can be messy at times. We've had our doubters, in addition to our own doubts, about what we're doing. And we've tried a number of things that simply didn't work for one reason or another. Of course, from time to time our own egos and time constraints have gotten in the way of our relationships.

Here are just a few of our discoveries:

We've learned that it is hard to give up pontificating or seeing every encounter as an opportunity to teach young people something. On one occasion, Donna's daughter, at the age of thirteen, said to her, "Just be quiet. Just listen to what I have to say. If I can just talk about it, I'll figure it out for myself." These powerful comments established Donna's style for sincerely listening and staying open to what young people have to say.

Another thing we've learned is that to have a meaningful conversation with young people, we need to give them our full attention—to look them in the eyes as we're visiting. Too often our interactions, especially at home, take place when we are doing other things that distract us from really listening—making dinner, setting the table, reading the paper, writing a note.

However, not being present happens outside the home as well. At receptions and gatherings with youth and adults, we've seen adults scanning the room to determine who else they want to connect with at the same time they are talking to a young person.

And while we're listening, we've learned to look for key phrases. It helps to keep the mind attentive to what really is being said rather than letting our minds wander, and hearing only what we want to hear. We've learned that if we're continually thinking about how we are going to respond, we're not really listening. We also have learned to be attentive to body language, young people's and our own. It often expresses much more than mere words.

When we are engaging youth in our meetings, we've learned the difficult lesson of finding a balance between our commitment to the agenda and the meeting time allowed and giving youth enough time to express their ideas and opinions. Often they need the extra time, especially if they are new to the leadership experience. Build it into the agenda.

Do you recall the song from the musical *South Pacific,* "You've Got to Be Carefully Taught"? The first line goes like this: "You've got to be taught to hate and fear." Well, we've learned that young people sometimes come to us with preconceived ideas and negative stereotypes about race, culture, gender, and justice that they learned from their parents and other family or community members. We've learned that while we work to provide experiences to broaden their world and perspective and critical thinking skills, we can't teach them what to think or what to say. In the final analysis, that's up to them.

We've learned to set high expectations, but also that we need to move slowly to earn the trust of young people.

We've also learned that we need to develop the necessary cultural competency to work with youth and their families who come from backgrounds different from our own. For example, thinking that all young people love to dance, we offered a dance after an event to encourage teens to bond with each other. Unfortunately, because of religious and gender identifications, not all felt comfortable participating. We've learned the importance of really knowing the young people in our group, what is right for them or not right for them, to engage them in decision making and to offer attractive alternatives. One size does not fit all.

We've learned to set high expectations, but also that we need to move slowly to earn the trust of young people. Jackie worked with a group in an after-school program for ten months before they decided to trust her. They learned by small experiences that she followed through and did what she said she was going to do. It took a long time for confidence to take shape!

We've learned that despite our belief that we "bring" young people to various leadership activities, they are quick to remind us that no matter how many incentives we provide, no matter how much we try to motivate them, no matter how much support and encouragement we give, *it's still their choice.* They are the ones who ultimately decide if they will come. Now that is a humbling realization! Despite it, we always invite; we always encourage.

And sadly, when checking with government agencies that we knew had youth advisories in the past, we learned that changes in administrations and budgets too often led to the elimination of this critical element. And too often, youth are authentically involved only because of one person's commitment. Then, when that person leaves, no new champion steps forward. As adults concerned about giving voice to the leader within our young people, we need to work toward a sustainable integration of youth as leaders in all local and state government agencies and advocate for continuity when change occurs.

As young people express and share their voice and ideas, we've learned the importance of following through. If we don't, the young people are likely to ask, "Why bother?" If we don't intend to use their comments and ideas, why did we ask for input in the first place? If we can't utilize their idea, create a dialogue that explores the reason why. You might talk about uncertainty as part of life, but you don't want to promise what you know cannot happen. When we give young people their voice and action is taken, we have an impact on both policy and the systems in which they are engaged.

A final lesson learned—in addition to a good sense of humor and a promise not to take ourselves so seriously—is the following. Before inviting young people on a trip, engage them in establishing and agreeing to ground rules and consequences for behavior. For example, boys cannot be in girls' rooms, and vice versa, nor can a couple go off on their own. They can be together in public places, but if they are found in the wrong rooms, their parents are called, and they must return home. Other ground rules might involve alcohol, drugs, tobacco, and curfews. Reaching an agreement on times for check-ins with adults is also critical.

Setting ground rules in advance saves adults from the very difficult task of reprimanding a student when they think something has gone wrong. In our experience, not knowing the rules in advance can ruin a relationship.

A Final Word: The Mark of a True Leader

We are well aware that not everyone finds working with young people her or his life's work. However, all of us can have an impact, in small ways, on the young people in our lives. We trust that readers will find in our comments and experiences an example or two that will strengthen their own relationships.

Leadership is a process, not an event. Each day we learn something new about carrying out our own leadership responsibilities. Each day we see new opportunities to connect with young people in positive ways.

Sometimes we need to take the time to look, as well as to listen. Not all the young people described in these pages would have initially been identified as having leadership potential. If a young person says no to your invitation and you want to pursue the opportunity, go back and assess what it would take for yes to be the response. What didn't he or she like about what you offered? What incentive would make acceptance more likely? How can you redefine the opportunity so that it makes sense?

Leadership is a process, not an event.

Some of the young leaders who became an important part of our activities came literally "off the streets." But, oh, what a difference they've learned to make! And what a difference they've made in our lives. It's both awesome and awe-inspiring. It changes lives. The journey with young people feeds our spirit and makes us fully alive. And the journey continues.

Reflections—Your Thoughts and Inspirations

Taking time to reflect on our experiences deepens our learning. It fosters critical thinking and analysis. Use the following suggestions to gain new insight into your own experiences, articulate them in writing, and apply that awareness to connect more effectively with young people.

1. Leadership, like teaching and learning, is a two-way street. How did a young person inspire you to give voice to the leader within you? Name specific attributes that you can, in turn, pass on to someone else.

   _____

   _____

   _____

   _____

   _____

2. Recall a time when an adult provided an opportunity for you to express your voice. How did that make you feel valued? What was the outcome?

   _____

   _____

   _____

   _____

   _____

3. How do your connections to community projects and issues contribute to the sense that you have a stake in the community? How does that relate to further action on your part?

   _____

   _____

   _____

   _____

   _____

4. Have you ever stood out on an issue alone? How did you feel? Who supported you? How was that different than being part of a larger group speaking out? Which was more comfortable? Why? Was it worth it?

_____

_____

_____

_____

_____

5. Recall a time that you worked cooperatively on a project. How would it have been different if you had been in competition with someone?

_____

_____

_____

_____

_____

Leadership Activities—Your Actions

For each of the activities described below, determine what specific steps you will take to complete the activity, a timeline for doing so, and a statement or two about what you hope to accomplish by completing the activity. Finally, indicate what resources you'll need to make it happen.

1. Encourage youth to write stories of how sharing their voice and being a leader has impacted their lives. Share the stories with your local newspaper, radio, or cable TV.

Action Steps:

Timeline:

Desired Outcomes:

Resources:

2. Along with youth, plan and host a "spoken-word" event about giving voice to the leader within and the impact it can have on individuals. Invite the school or the public library or city hall to create a venue for the event.

Action Steps:

Timeline:

Desired Outcomes:

Resources:

_____

_____

3. Create, along with a group of young people, a poster contest to capture their vision of the impact of authentic leadership. Or you can simply do this as an activity during one of your meetings or a retreat.

Action Steps:

_____

Timeline:

_____

Desired Outcomes:

_____

Resources:

_____

4. Design, with a group of young people, a campaign that supports what they need from adults, namely, opportunities, resources, space, trust, honesty, support. Give voice to their ideas on a parade float, booth at the county fair, conference, city festival, or neighborhood gathering.

Action Steps:

Timeline:

Desired Outcomes:

Resources:

5. Work with a group of young people to design a leadership development activity in which each one will partner with a younger person to pass the leadership baton to yet another, thereby ensuring continuity in an organization.

Action Steps:

Timeline:

Desired Outcomes:

Resources:

_____

_____

6. Talk with young leaders about the significance of shaking hands. Then work with them to develop and practice strong, confident handshakes.

_____

Action Steps:

_____

Timeline:

_____

Desired Outcomes:

_____

Resources:

_____

Actions—Your Afterthoughts

After you've carried out each activity or its modification, reflect on the experience using the following guide.

1. What happened when I tried this?

_____

_____

_____

2. What did I learn?

_____

_____

_____

3. What changes will I make the next time I try it?

_____

_____

_____

4. How did these actions help young people to give voice to the leader within?

_____

_____

_____

Acknowledgments

This book is dedicated to all the young people who enrich our lives and renew our spirits. We strive together in leading our organizations and communities for positive change.

Our special gratitude to the young people who shared their wisdom and their stories with us and gave us permission to showcase their experiences in our book:

Erko Abdullahi
Salina Atlas
Maya Babu
Frannie Boehnlein
Kyle Bushyhead
Samantha
   Christensen
Michael Elliot

Kristine Engel
Will Gaines
Haley Gunderson
Jack Gunderson
Matt Knutson
Eric Minter
Kristi Pell
Mike Radmer

Jamie Seitzer
Callie Tabor
Struther Van Horn
Paul Vulcan
Hannah Westre
Via Yang

Our deepest appreciation to the following people for their guidance, support, editorial expertise, and permission to use their words to help tell our story:

Pastor Alan Bray
Heather Erickson
Cindy Freeman
Brent Gillen
Heather Gillen
Peter Gillen
Rabbi Simeon
   Glaser

Linda Hall
Christopher
   Johnson
H. Stuart Johnson
Alex Metchnek
Nicky Metchnek
Abdul Mohamed
Anne Parish

Sue Peterson
Holly Phillips
Liz Power-
   Hawkinson
Polly Roach
Stephen Sinykin
Dede Strom

About the Authors

As a young person, **Donna C. Gillen** *(left)* was involved in leadership and service activities that led to her lifelong goal to create similar opportunities for other young people. On her career path over the past forty years, Donna has enjoyed creating opportunities for young people and families to be engaged in leadership roles to solve community concerns. She has received state and national awards for her work with youth and families. A strong advocate for authentic youth-adult partnerships, Donna is a champion on local, state, and national levels for youth voice and youth leadership for all young people. Currently the executive director of youthrive (the host organization of Upper Midwest Affiliate of PeaceJam International), she is passionate about supporting emerging young leaders.

Marlys C. Johnson *(right)* is a retired national nonprofit executive with a lifelong commitment to leadership, children, youth, and communities. A former educator and director of a Big Sisters organization, Marlys has designed a number of programs that benefit young people, including ScholarShop, a curriculum to motivate and prepare students for postsecondary education. With corporate and foundation partners, she has established a wide variety of student aid and scholarship programs that offer young people access to higher education. She has provided leadership on the boards of state and national organizations dedicated to young people and founded several youth-related programs in her community. In addition to championing young people from all walks of life, Marlys currently works as a consultant to nonprofits, a workshop leader and trainer, and a visiting professor at Gustavus Adolphus College.

One constant throughout **Jackie S. Sinykin**'s *(center)* multiple careers has been young people. As a speech therapist-audiologist practicing clinically and in middle schools, Jackie's focus was working with youth to build greater self-assurance while improving speech. Many of her current ideas about youth leadership are a result of volunteering in youth-serving organizations while raising three children. As executive director of a community volunteer center, Jackie's leadership direction focused on promoting broad-based opportunities and support for youth and family community involvement. Today, she consults with nonprofit organizations, facilitates strategic planning, presents trainings and workshops, and is an executive coach for the University of St. Thomas, Center for Nonprofit Management Institute for Executive Director Leadership.

If you are interested in an interactive workshop or training for your organization or conference, based on the four primary dimensions of youth leadership engagement illustrated in **Giving Voice to the Leader Within**, *contact:*

Marlys C. Johnson at 507-934-1878 or mcjcsfa@aol.com.

To order additional copies of *Giving Voice to the Leader Within*

Web:	www.itascabooks.com
Phone:	1-800-901-3480
Fax:	Copy and fill out the form below with credit card information. Fax to 763-398-0198.
Mail:	Copy and fill out the form below. Mail with check or credit card information to:

Syren Book Company
5120 Cedar Lake Road
Minneapolis, MN 55416

ORDER FORM

Copies	Title / Author	Price	Totals
	Giving Voice to the Leader Within / Donna C. Gillen, Marlys C. Johnson, & Jackie S. Sinykin	$15.95	$
	Subtotal		$
	7% sales tax (MN only)		$
	Shipping and handling, first copy		$ 4.00
	Shipping and handling, ___ add'l copies @$1.00 ea.		$
	TOTAL TO REMIT		$

PAYMENT INFORMATION:

__ Check Enclosed __ Visa/MasterCard		
Card number:	Expiration date:	
Name on card:		
Billing address:		
City:	State:	Zip:
Signature:	Date:	

SHIPPING INFORMATION:

__ Same as billing address __ Other (enter below)		
Name:		
Address:		
City:	State:	Zip: